Gaynor Ramsey

Non-Stop English 1

Interkantonale Lehrmittelzentrale
Lehrmittelverlag des Kantons Zürich

Lehrmittel der Interkantonalen Lehrmittelzentrale

CD Texts and Dialogues (1:1 = CD 1:Track 1)
CD Home Practice Selected Texts (2 = Track Nr.)

Beraterteam
Kurt Bannwart (Vorsitz)
Peter Aisslinger
Fritz Egolf
Ernst Maurer

Experte
Eugen Hefti

Projektleiter Buchherstellung: Jakob Sturzenegger
Grafische Gestaltung: Hans Rudolf Ziegler
Illustrationen: Bob Harvey, Martin Shovel, Marianne Sinner
Fotos: William Godfrey, Susann Tweitmann-Sperb
Bildnachweis: 'Britain on View' – The British Tourist Authority, London (pages 13, 133)
    Claire Winstone, Canvey Island (page 32)
    Eurocentres, Zurich (page 32)
    The Tourist Office, St. Moritz (pages 128, 133)
    Davstone Holdings Ltd, Land's End – for The First and Last House in England (page 133)
Umschlag: Hubert Hasler

© Lehrmittelverlag des Kantons Zürich
16. Ausgabe 2010, unverändert (2009)
Printed in Switzerland
ISBN 978-3-906718-80-4
www.lehrmittelverlag.com

Contents

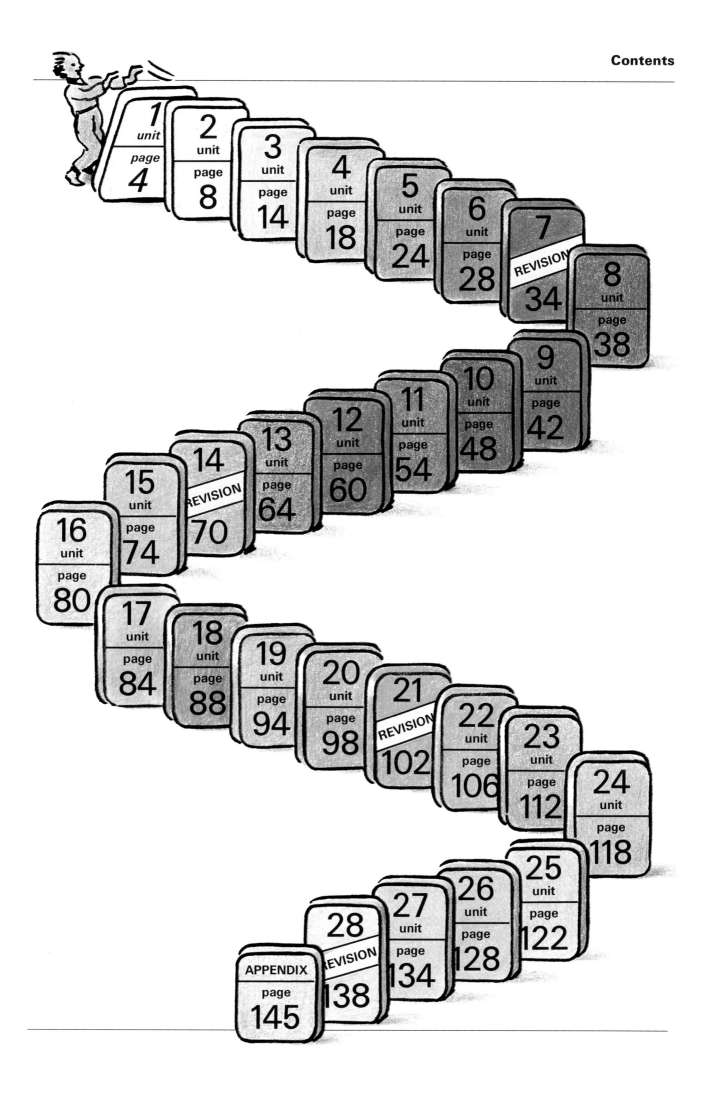

Unit one – the first unit in this book!

1

◉ 1:1
◉ 2

The International Centre is in Wales. It's a centre for students. It's the first day of the international summer camp. Belinda is from Wales, and she's the receptionist at the centre.

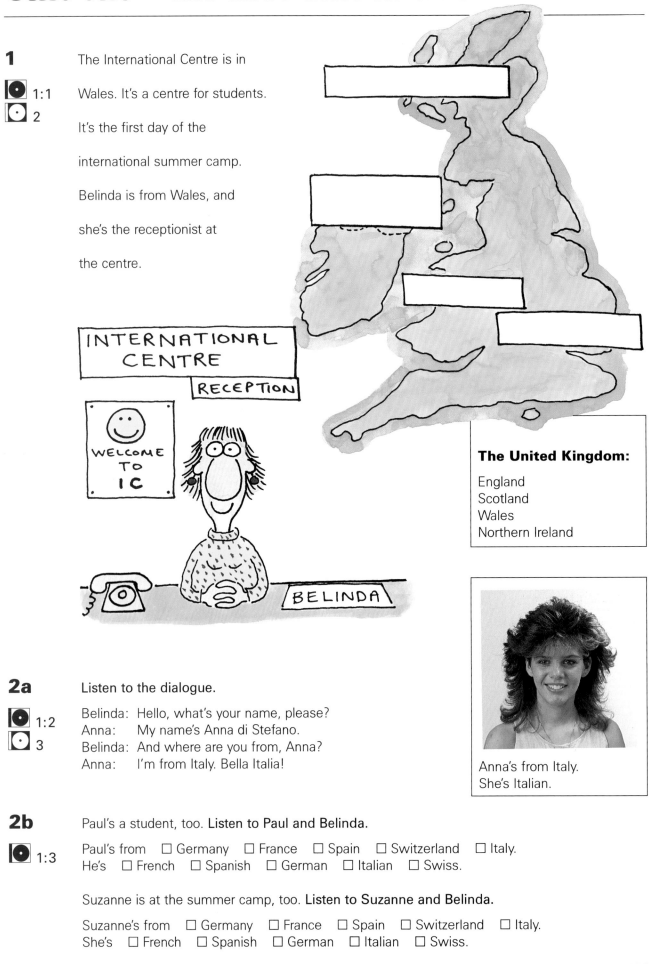

The United Kingdom:

England
Scotland
Wales
Northern Ireland

Anna's from Italy.
She's Italian.

2a   Listen to the dialogue.

◉ 1:2
◉ 3

Belinda: Hello, what's your name, please?
Anna: My name's Anna di Stefano.
Belinda: And where are you from, Anna?
Anna: I'm from Italy. Bella Italia!

2b   Paul's a student, too. **Listen to Paul and Belinda.**

◉ 1:3

Paul's from ☐ Germany ☐ France ☐ Spain ☐ Switzerland ☐ Italy.
He's ☐ French ☐ Spanish ☐ German ☐ Italian ☐ Swiss.

Suzanne is at the summer camp, too. **Listen to Suzanne and Belinda.**

Suzanne's from ☐ Germany ☐ France ☐ Spain ☐ Switzerland ☐ Italy.
She's ☐ French ☐ Spanish ☐ German ☐ Italian ☐ Swiss.

2c   Listen to the tape and complete these sentences:

🔘 1:4   *e.g. Anna's from* _____*Italy*_____ , *she's* _____*Italian*_____ .

Cristina's from _____ , she's _____ .

Peter's from _____ , he's _____ .

Maria's from _____ , she's _____ .

Robert's from _____ , he's _____ .

Tony's from _____ , he's _____ .

3a   **Where's she from? Where's he from?** Cristina, Tony, Paul, Peter, and Anna

Cristina
Spain

Belinda
Britain

3b   **The colours of the flags** – the British flag is red, white and blue.

	black	blue	green	red	white	yellow
France						
Germany						
Italy						
Spain						
Switzerland						

3c   Look at these sentences:

e.g. Belinda's from Britain. The British flag is red, white and blue.

Write sentences about   a) Cristina   b) Tony   c) Paul   d) Peter   e) Anna

4a   What's the answer?

Is the International Centre in Wales?	Yes, it is. / No, it isn't.
Is the French flag red, white and green?	Yes, it is. / No, it isn't.
Is Belinda a receptionist?	Yes, she is. / No, she isn't.
Is Anna from Germany?	Yes, she is. / No, she isn't.
Is Peter Spanish?	Yes, he is. / No, he isn't.
Is Tony from France?	Yes, he is. / No, he isn't.

4b   Write these sentences:

e.g. International Centre / Wales   *The International Centre is in Wales.*
    Anna / Germany   *Anna isn't from Germany.*

a) French flag / red, white and green   d) Tony / France
b) Belinda / a receptionist   e) International Centre / Scotland
c) Peter / Spanish   f) Anna / Italian

4c   Write questions and short answers:

e.g. Belinda / British?   *Is Belinda British?*   *Yes, she is.*
    Belinda / Scotland?   *Is Belinda from Scotland?*   *No, she isn't.*

a) Wales / the United Kingdom?   d) Swiss flag / blue and white?
b) Belinda / Wales?   e) Paul / German?
c) Suzanne / Spain?   f) Peter / Spanish?

5a Make a dialogue.

 1:5

Belinda   Tony

| Hello. |

| What's your name? |

| And where are you from? |

| Oh, are you from Paris? |

Tony's words:

It's Tony.   From France.
No, I'm not, I'm from Avignon. Hello.

5b **Make some more dialogues:** Belinda and Peter, Belinda and Anna, Belinda and…

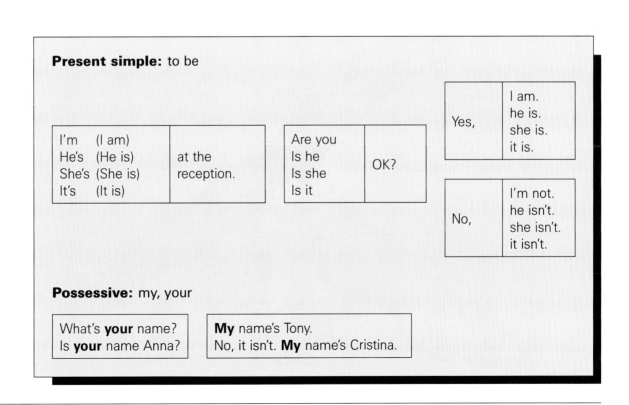

Present simple: to be

I'm (I am)	
He's (He is)	at the
She's (She is)	reception.
It's (It is)	

Are you	
Is he	
Is she	OK?
Is it	

Yes,	I am.
	he is.
	she is.
	it is.

No,	I'm not.
	he isn't.
	she isn't.
	it isn't.

Possessive: my, your

| What's **your** name? | **My** name's Tony. |
| Is **your** name Anna? | No, it isn't. **My** name's Cristina. |

Unit two – the second unit

1a Listen to Belinda.

🔘 1:6
🔘 4

Hello everybody. Welcome to summer camp. My name's Belinda and I'm the receptionist here. This is a plan of the camp. This is tent A, this is tent B and this is tent C. Tents D and E are here, next to the reception. This is the snack bar, next to the entrance…

"Belinda, excuse me …. where are the toilets, please?"

Oh yes, sorry! They're here …. toilets and washrooms for the boys are here, and for the girls …. here, OK?

1b   **What's this?**

e.g. What's this?   *It's the reception.*

What _____ ?   It's a _____.

_____ *this* ?   It's the _____.

_____ *'s* ?   It's the _____.

_____ ?   It's a _____.

1c

🔘 1:7

Listen to the tape. Where are the students, in tent A, B, C or D?
Belinda is in tent E.

Anna _____   Suzanne _____   Peter _____   Robert _____

Paul _____   Cristina _____   Maria _____   Tony _____

Complete these sentences:

Paul and _____ are in tent ___ .   Cristina ___ in tent B with _____ .

Robert and Tony _____ in _____ C.   Belinda ___ ___ tent E.

Anna _____ _____ _____ in tent ___ .

1d

Where are they? Where is he? Where is she?

e.g. Where is Belinda?   *She's in tent E.*
*   Where are Peter and Paul?*   *They're in tent A.*

a) Anna   b) Cristina and Maria   c) Peter   d) Robert and Tony   e) Suzanne

2a

Match the questions and answers.

a) Is Belinda from Wales?   No, I'm not.
b) Are Cristina and Maria in tent B?   Yes, they are.
c) Is the snack bar next to the washrooms?   *a)* Yes, she is.
d) Is Belinda a student?   No, it isn't.
e) Are tents D and E next to the snack bar?   Yes, I am.
f) Is the summer camp for students?   No, she isn't.
g) Are you a student?   Yes, it is.
h) Are you on Unit 1 of this book?   No, they aren't.

2b

Where is ...? Where are ....?

e.g. Where is Belinda's tent?   *It's next to the reception.*
*   Where are Robert and Tony?*   *They're in tent C.*

a) the snack bar   b) Belinda   c) the camp   d) Cristina and Maria   e) tent D   f) the reception

2c

🔘 1:8
🔘 5
🎭

Make a dialogue.

A: Excuse me, where's tent A?
B: I'm sorry – I don't know.
A: Oh. Excuse me, where's tent A?
C: It's here, next to tent B.
A: Thank you.

Ask about:

tent B   the reception   Belinda's tent   the snack bar   the entrance   tent C

3a

🔘 1:9

It's the first evening at the camp.
The students are in the snack bar.
Listen.

Suzanne's photo

Now listen to Tony, Maria and Robert.
Write the names under the photos:

3b

🔘 1:10

Listen again. Are these words in Tony's dialogue?

photo ✔	garden	school
friend	hotel	car

3c

🔘 1:11

Listen to Maria's dialogue. Number these words in the correct order.

teacher _____   class _____1_____   film _____   classroom _____

4a

Robert's in the snack bar.
What's on the tray?

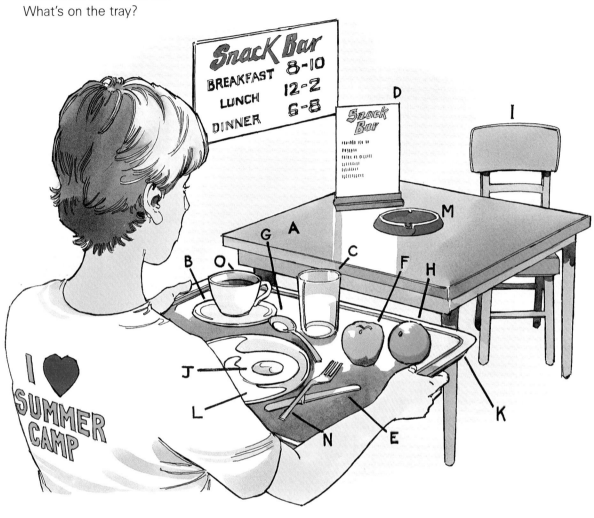

a tray [K]	a cup ☐	a saucer ☐	a knife ☐	an ashtray ☐
a fork ☐	a menu ☐	a plate ☐	a table ☐	an egg ☐
a glass ☐	a spoon ☐	a chair ☐	an apple ☐	an orange ☐

4b

What's .... ? It's a ... .

e.g. What's this?   – *It's a cup.*
    What's L?   – *It's a plate.*
    Is E a spoon?   – *No, it isn't. It's a knife.*

Present tense: to be

I'm	(I am)		Am I		in
You're	(You are)		Are you		tent
He's	(He is)		Is he		A?
She's	(She is)	in	Is she	in	
It's	(It is)	tent	Is it		
		F.			
We're	(We are)		Are we		
You're	(You are)		Are you		
They're	(They are)		Are they		

Yes,	I am.
	you are.
	he is.
	she is.
	it is.
	we are.
	you are.
	they are.

No,	I'm not.
	you aren't.
	he isn't.
	she isn't.
	it isn't.
	we aren't.
	you aren't.
	they aren't.

Indefinite article: a, an

What's this?

It's **an** ashtray.
an + a, e, i, o, u

It's **a** glass.
a + b, c, d, f .... z

The capital cities:

1. Trafalgar Square, London, England
2. The Grand Opera, Belfast, Northern Ireland
3. Calton Hill, Edinburgh, Scotland
4. The Town Hall, Cardiff, Wales

Unit three – the third unit

1a A new receptionist

The International Park Hotel is in London. The manager, Mr Pinzelli, must find a new receptionist. Three people are at the hotel for an interview.
Listen to the interviews.
What can Mary, Pat and Jane do? What can't they do?

 1:12

Mary	Pat	Jane	
			can speak French.
			can speak German.
			can speak Italian.
✓			can type.
			can write shorthand.
			can drive a car.
			can start next month.

1b Can Mary type? Can Pat write shorthand?

e.g. Can Mary type?   *Yes, she can.*
Can Pat write shorthand?   *No, he can't.*

1c What can they do? What can't they do? Write about Pat and Jane.

e.g. Mary can type, and she can write shorthand.
Mary can't speak German, and she can't drive a car.

2a

Work in groups of 5. Ask *Can you ....?* Write the information here with a tick (✓) or a cross (✗).

Names:	ride a bicycle	use a computer	play football	sing	ski	speak Italian	make coffee	cook spaghetti

2b

Make a report.

e.g. Three students in the group can ride a bicycle and two can't.

3a

Write sentences with these words:

e.g. can't ski   she   my sister   but   can swim
My sister can swim, but she can't ski.

a)   but   can't fly   a goldfish   can swim   it

b)   it   but   can't speak   can cry   a baby

c)   I   I   but   can ...   can't ...

d)   can ...   he / she   but   my friend   can't ...

e)   English   can speak   but   he / she   my teacher   can't speak ...

3b

Look at 2a. Write a sentence with *can* and a sentence with *can't* for each person in the group.

e.g. .... can type, and she can sing.
.... can ski, but she can't speak Italian.

3c

Can she ...? Can he ...? Can you ....?

e.g. Mary can type very well. (✱✱✱)
She can do shorthand, but not very well. (✱✱)
She can sing, but badly. (✱)
She can't speak French. (O)

What can Mary do? What can Pat do? What can Jane do? What can you do?

	speak German	type	do shorthand	speak French	ski	sing	play football	speak Italian
Mary	O	✱✱✱	✱✱	O	O	✱	✱	O
Pat	✱	✱✱✱	O	✱✱✱	✱	O	✱✱	✱✱✱
Jane	✱	✱✱✱	✱✱	✱✱	✱✱	✱✱	O	✱
you								

4a

What can they do? What can't they do?

Albert's blind.   Caroline's a baby.   Fred's in hospital.

		walk in the park.
Albert		watch television.
	can	phone a friend.
		read the newspaper.
Caroline		smile at people.
		eat fish and chips in a restaurant.
	can't	dance.
Fred		drive a car.
		cook spaghetti.

4b

Why ...? Because ...

e.g. Can Albert walk in the park?   *Yes, he can.*
Can Albert watch television?   *No, he can't.*
Why can't he watch television?   *Because he's blind.*

Ask and answer questions about Albert, Caroline and Fred.

5   Listen to the tape. Can you hear *can* or can you hear *can't* in the sentences?

🔴 1:13   CAN: _____   CAN'T: *1* _____

Present tense: can

I You He She (It) We You They	can can't	swim. type. ski.

Can	I you he she (it) we you they	swim? type? ski?

Yes,	I you he she (it) we you they	can.
No,		can't.

Why ...? Because ...

Why can't Albert drive a car? **Why** can't Caroline read the newspaper?

Because he's blind. **Because** she's a baby.

Adverbs: well, badly

He's a **good** tennis player. He's a **good** swimmer.	He can play tennis **well.** He can swim **well.**
He's a **bad** footballer. He's a **bad** singer.	He can play football, but **badly.** He can sing, but **badly.**

Unit four – the fourth unit

1a

1:14
6

Pat Johnson is the new receptionist at the International Park Hotel in London.
He's in the coffee bar with Anne, one of the secretaries at the hotel.

Anne: Are you from London, Pat?
Pat: No, I'm not …
I'm from Manchester.
My brothers and sisters are all in Manchester.
Anne: How many brothers and sisters have you got?
Pat: I've got three brothers and two sisters.
Anne: That's a big family, isn't it?
I've only got one sister.
Pat: And brothers?
Anne: No, none … one sister, that's all!

1b **How many brothers have you got, Jane? How many sisters have you got, John?**

John: Fred: Jane:

Ask three people in your class:

	John	Fred	Jane			
brothers	2	0	1			
sisters	1	0	0			
only child		✓				

1c   **How many brothers has he got? How many sisters has she got?**

How many brothers has John got?	He's got two.
How _____ sisters has John got?	He's _____ one.
Is John an only child?	No, he _____ .
_____ _____ brothers has Fred got?	None.
How many sisters _____ Fred _____?	_____ .
Is Fred _____ only _____?	_____ , _____ is.
How many brothers _____ Jane _____?	She's _____ one.
_____ _____ sisters _____ Jane _____?	_____ .
____ Jane an _____ _____ ?	_____ , _____ _____ .

2a   **John's family tree**

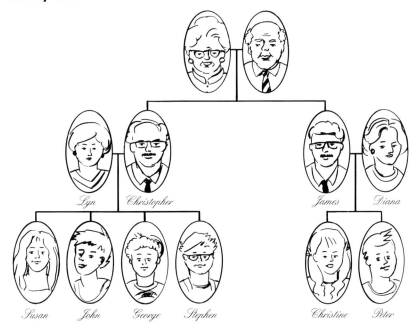

Make sentences about John's family.

e.g. sister: Susan is John's sister

    mother   wife   daughter   sister   aunt   cousin

    father   husband   son   brother   uncle   cousin

2b

Susan's got an aunt, she's called Diana.
Susan's got three brothers, they're called John, George and Stephen.

Write two sentences about Christopher, Christine and John.

2c

What's the answer? Look at exercise 2a.

Has John got two brothers?	Yes, he has.	/	No, he hasn't.
Have James and Diana got two sons?	Yes, they have.	/	No, they haven't.
Has Susan got a cousin called Christine?	Yes, she has.	/	No, she hasn't.
Have Lyn and Christopher got 3 daughters?	Yes, they have.	/	No, they haven't.
Have you got a sister?	Yes, I have.	/	No, I haven't.
Has your teacher got a brother?	Yes, _____ has.	/	No, _____ hasn't.

Has Christopher got a sister?

Have John and George got a brother?

Have you got a brother?

Has Susan got two cousins?

2d

Write about John's family.

e.g. John / a sister   *John's got a sister.*
John / 3 brothers   *John hasn't got three brothers.*
James and Diana / 2 sons   *James and Diana haven't got two sons.*

a) Lyn and Christopher / 2 daughters
b) Christine and Peter / 4 cousins
c) Lyn / a husband called Peter
d) James and Diana / one son
e) Christopher / a sister

f) James / a wife called Lyn
g) Peter / 2 sisters
h) Peter and Christine / a sister
i) Susan / 3 brothers
j) James and Diana / 2 sons

3

Listen and answer the questions.

1:15   a) Has the receptionist at the International Park Hotel got a room?

1. _yes_   2. _____   3. _____   4. _____   5. _____   6. _____

1:16   b) Has he or she got a Rolls Royce?

1. _____   2. _____   3. _____   4. _____   5. _____   6. _____

1:17   c) Has he or she got the English book?

1. _____   2. _____   3. _____   4. _____   5. _____   6. _____

4

 1:18

a) Listen and write the numbers that you hear.

A: _____   B: _____   C: _____

D: _____   E: _____   F: _____

 1:19

b) Which numbers can you hear? **Listen to the example.**

e.g. 0 ① *2* ③ ④ *5* ⑥ ⑦ *8* ⑨

A: 0 1 2 3 4 5 6 7 8 9   B: 0 1 2 3 4 5 6 7 8 9   C: 0 1 2 3 4 5 6 7 8 9

D: 0 one two three four five six seven eight nine

E: 0 one two three four five six seven eight nine

F: 0 one two three four five six seven eight nine

5   **How many cars can you see? Can you see seven watches?**

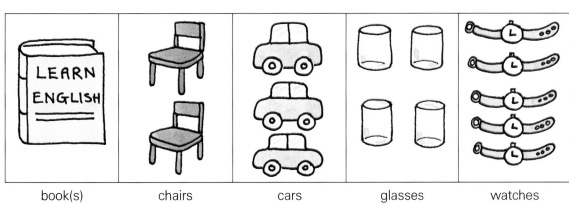

book(s)   chairs   cars   glasses   watches

men   women   children   babies

e.g. How many glasses can you see?   *I can see four.*
Can you see three chairs?   *No, I can't. I can only see two.*

Present tense: have got

			got	a computer.
I've	(have)			
You've	(have)			
He's	(has)			
She's	(has)			
It's	(has)			
We've	(have)			
You've	(have)			
They've	(have)			

	got	a computer?
(Have I)		
Have you		
Has he		
Has she		
Has it		
(Have we)		
Have you		
Have they		

Yes,	I have. (you have.) he has. she has. it has. we have. (you have.) they have.

No,	I haven't. (you haven't.) he hasn't. she hasn't. it hasn't. we haven't. (you haven't.) they haven't.

Nouns: singular and plural

singular	plural
computer	computers
chair	chairs
car	cars
gla**ss**	glass**es**
wat**ch**	watch**es**
bab**y**	bab**ies**
secretar**y**	secretar**ies**
man	men
woman	women
child	children

Genitive: 's

Susan is John**'s** sister.
John is Susan**'s** brother.

Places to eat:

1. A potato stand in a market
2. A pub
3. A snack bar
4. An elegant restaurant
5. A self-service restaurant
6. A fish-and-chip shop
7. A sandwich bar

Unit five – the fifth unit

1a   Bill is an interviewer for Radio One One One.

Listen to this interview with Jeanine. She's

a pop singer. Who's her favourite singer?

What's her favourite colour?

1:20

singer	colour	city	drink	food	film star
☐ Frank Sinatra	☐ red	☐ Paris	☐ coffee	☐ Italian	☐ Charlie Chaplin
☐ Mona	☐ blue	☐ London	☐ tea	☐ French	☐ Sophia Loren
☐ The Beatles	☐ green	☐ New York	☐ wine	☐ English	☐ Dustin Hoffman
☐ Elvis Presley	☐ black	☐ Zurich	☐ beer	☐ Spanish	☐ Bo Derek

1b   Write the missing words:

Who _is_ Jeanine?   She's ____ pop singer.

What's her favourite _____ ?   Black.

_____ ____ _____ city?   _____ _____ .

_____ ____ favourite _____ ?   Tea.

What's _____ _____ _____ ?   Spanish food.

___ Frank Sinatra her _____ _____ ?   No, ____ _____ .

Who's _____ _____ film star?   _____ _____ .

1c   Here are Bill's answers to "What's your favourite …?": beer, Jeanine, French, Bo Derek, London and green. **Write six sentences about Bill beginning** *His favourite …*

1d   **What's your favourite …? Who's your favourite …?**

Ask your partner about his or her favourite singer, colour, city, drink, food and film star. Can you find two other things to ask?

2 Bill and Jeanine

	long	short	black	red	blue	white
hair	J	B	J	B		
pullover						
shoes						
trousers						

a) *e.g. His hair is short and her hair is long.*
    His trousers are short and her trousers are long.

b) **Write five questions** – the answers must be negative.

   e.g. Is his hair long?   *No, it isn't.*
        Are his trousers long?   *No, they aren't.*

3

Listen to the tape and match the numbers to the people in the picture.

4 Make a dialogue.

A: Can you give me John's book please?

B: Is this his book?

A: Yes, I think so.

B: Here you are.

A: Thank you.

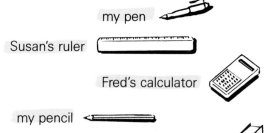

my pen

Susan's ruler

Fred's calculator

my pencil

Barbara's rubber   Peter's dictionary

5 Write these five sentences – start with the name.

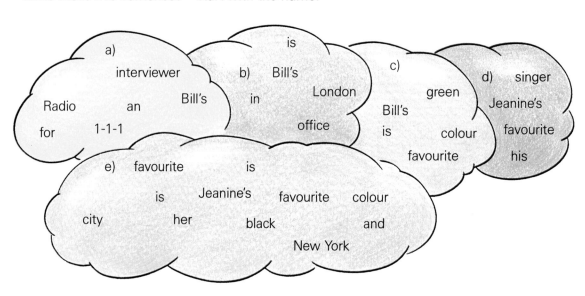

a) interviewer   Bill's   Radio   an   for   1-1-1

b) is   Bill's   in   London   office

c) Bill's   green   is   colour   favourite

d) singer   Jeanine's   favourite   his

e) favourite   is   is   Jeanine's   favourite   colour   city   her   black   and   New York

6a 's ≠ 's ≠ 's

e.g. *Bill's got an office.* = *Bill has got an office.*
Bill's office is in London. = *His office is in London.*
Bill's in his office. = *Bill is in his office.*

Write these sentences with no 's.

Jeanine's mother is French.
Jeanine's got a house in New York.
Jeanine's a singer.

Fred's got an Italian car.
It's in the garden.
Fred's car is black and red.

Susan's a student.
Susan's got an English dictionary.
Susan's dictionary is on the table.

HEY, WHAT ARE WE ?

6b Listen. Is the **'s** *has got, his / her* or *is?*

 1:23

	1	2	3	4	5	6	7	8
has got								
his / her								
is								

Possessive: his, her

I'm a receptionist and	**my**	hotel		Zurich.
You're a student and	**your**	school	is in	Paris.
He's an interviewer and	**his**	office		London.
She's a singer and	**her**	family		New York.

Apostrophe: 's

's	's	's
He**'s got** a car.	Bill**'s** mother is here.	He**'s** in London.
He **has got** a car.	(the mother **of Bill**)	He **is** in London.
She**'s got** two sisters.	Jane**'s** hair is long.	She**'s** a student.
She **has got** two sisters.	(the hair **of Jane**)	She **is** a student.

Unit six – the sixth unit

1a   Bill and his wife, Maggie, are in London. They are at the cinema.

🔲 1:24

🔲 8

Bill: What time is the film, please?
Lady: 5 o'clock and 8 o'clock, sir.
Bill: 5 o'clock? That's good. Can I have two
        tickets for 5 o'clock, please?
Lady: £3, £4 or £5?
Bill: Erm … £4, please.
Lady: OK, here you are – that's £8, please.
Bill: Thank you.

Info 2009:
Cinema tickets in London
cost a lot more now – they
can be up to £18 in big,
modern cinemas.

1b   **Make dialogues with this information.** Remember – *please* and *thank you* are very important
           words in English.

concert	**?** o'clock	**?** tickets	£7 per ticket
opera	o'clock	tickets	£9 per ticket
play	o'clock	tickets	£8 per ticket

1c   Correct the information here:

e.g. Bill's in Manchester today.   *No, he isn't, he's in London.*

1. Bill's with his mother.
2. Bill and his wife are at the opera.
3. Bill's got a wife called Suzie.
4. Their tickets are £10.
5. They've got three tickets for 8 o'clock.
6. The film is at 6 o'clock.

2a

🔊 1:25

In the film, two children and two green men are in a park. **Listen.**

Where are the green men from? ☐ Mars ☐ Venus ☐ Liverpool
Where are the green men now? ☐ London ☐ Liverpool ☐ Birmingham

Is it Tommy's sentence (T) or the green man's sentence (GM)?

1) Where are we? _____

2) Where are you from? _____

3) Our names are 12 and 14. _____

4) Our house is number 11. _____

5) Our houses are green. _____

6) Our language isn't English. _____

7) Our flag is red, white and blue. _____

2b This is a letter from Green Man 12 to his wife, Green Woman 17.
Write in the missing words.

DEAR GREENIE,
WE'RE IN BIRMINGHAM NOW. BIRMINGHAM IS VERY DIFFERENT.

GREENMANLAND

OUR MEN AND WOMEN ARE GREEN. OUR HOUSES
_____ . _____ FLAG IS
_____ . _____ ISN'T
ENGLISH. _____ NAMES _____ NUMBERS.
_____ FOOD _____ .

BIRMINGHAM

THEIR MEN AND WOMEN AREN'T GREEN. THEIR
_____ AREN'T _____ .
FLAG _____ .
LANGUAGE _____ .
NAMES _____ WORDS.
_____ FOOD IS DIFFERENT.

THEY ARE DIFFERENT, AREN'T THEY? HELLO TO OUR GREEN SON, A GREEN KISS, GM12

3

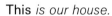

This *is our house.*   That *is their house.*

Write sentences beginning with *this* or *that.*

e.g. 1a. This is our car.
    1b. That is their car.

my / our	his / her / their	my / our	his / her / their
1a	1b	5a	5b
2a	2b	6a	6b
3a	3b	7a	7b
4a	4b	8a	8b

4a

1:26

9

Listen to these numbers:

1 2 3 4 5 6 7 8 9 10 11 12 13 14 15 16 17 18 19 20

Write in the words next to the numbers.

1. _____   6. _____   11. _____   16. _____

2. _____   7. _____   12. _____   17. _____

3. _____   8. _____   13. _____   18. _____

4. _____   9. _____   14. _____   19. _____

5. _____   10. _____   15. _____   20. _____

The words:
sixteen   four   ten   eight   nineteen   one   nine   eleven   fifteen   two   twenty
seven   fourteen   three   eighteen   six   seventeen   twelve   five   thirteen

4b

Write the numbers only.

 1:27

	Tommy	Caroline	George	Susan	Green Man 12
age	*12*				
house number	*11*				

5a

| this / these | that / those |

Write these sentences and questions in the plural:

e.g. This is my book.   *These are my books.*

1. Is that your book?   3. This is my chair.   5. That's their car.
2. That's John's shoe.   4. Is this my letter?   6. This isn't my photo.

5b

Make a dialogue.

 1:28
 10

A: Is this my letter?
B: Yes … oh, and that letter's for you, too.
A: Thanks.

book   pencil

letters   books

pencils   tickets

dictionary pen

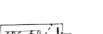

6a A letter from Claire

Sea View,
Victoria Road,
Stanton - Upon - Sea,
England . ST7 3YJ
Friday 10ᵀᴴ

Dear...,
    My name's Claire. I'm English. I can't speak German but I can speak a little French. I'm 14 years old, and I'm from Stanton-Upon-Sea, near London. I've got a brother and a sister. My favourite singer is Mona. Who is your favourite singer? I've got a penfriend in Canada, but I haven't got a penfriend in Europe. Can you be my penfriend? My hobbies are swimming, reading, playing tennis and listening to pop music.

Love,

Claire

6b Write to Claire.

Possessive: our, your, their

This is That's	**my** **your** **his** **her** **our** **your** **their**	television. car. house.

These are Those are	**my** **your** **his** **her** **our** **your** **their**	books. letters. friends.

Demonstrative pronouns: this, that, these, those

Is	**this** **that**	your laptop?	Yes, it is. No, it isn't.

Are	**these** **those**	your letters?	Yes, they are. No, they aren't.

Unit seven – the seventh unit

Revision unit

1a   Find Picasso's seven colours, across (→) or down (↓).

	1	2	3	4	5	6	7	8	9
11	w	s	j	t	x	a	f	g	i
12	k	d	p	i	c	a	s	s	o
13	l	h	b	d	b	l	a	c	k
14	a	o	r	a	n	g	e	y	w
15	r	j	e	c	m	r	y	e	h
16	a	k	d	l	h	e	a	l	i
17	n	d	b	l	u	e	n	l	t
18	x	u	s	m	v	n	f	o	e
19	z	o	t	r	w	p	u	w	g

1b   **'Number words'** – the numbers are ACROSS/DOWN in Picasso's colours (1a).

1:29   *e.g.   1/13   2/14   7/17   4/13   8/18   5/14   =   London*

Write the numbers you hear and then write the towns. Are the towns in England, Scotland, Wales or Ireland?

1. _/__ _/__ _/__ _/__ _/__ _/__ _/__   = _____

2. _/__ _/__ _/__ _/__ _/__ _/__   = _____

3. _/__ _/__ _/__ _/__ _/__ _/__ _/__   = _____

4. _/__ _/__ _/__ _/__ _/__ _/__ _/__   = _____

5. _/__ _/__ _/__ _/__   = _____

6. _/__ _/__ _/__ _/__ _/__ _/__ _/__ _/__   _/__

    = _____

1c   Make three 'number words' for your partner with the names of three people in your class.

2

My name's George and I'm from Manchester. My mother's French and my father's English. I've got one sister, but I haven't got a brother. I can speak French, because my mother's French, and I'm a student of German in London. I'm not in London today, I'm in Manchester with my friends.

Write in the missing words:

Her name's Mary and _____ from Birmingham. _____ mother's _____ and _____ father's _____ .

_____ _____ two sisters, but she _____ _____ a

brother. _____ _____ speak _____ , because her

mother's _____ , and _____ a student of

_____ in London. She _____ in London today,

_____ in Birmingham with _____ friends.

Now, for Fred and Suzie:

Their names _____ Fred and Suzie and _____ from

Liverpool. _____ mother's _____ and _____

father's _____ . _____ _____ one sister, but they

_____ _____ a brother. They _____ speak

_____ , because _____ mother's _____ , and

_____ _____ of German in London. _____

_____ in London today, _____ in Liverpool with

_____ friends.

3a

How many people (, and) can you see in these pictures?

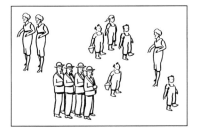

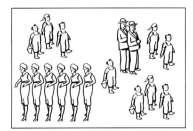

e.g. In the first picture I can see _____ _____ , _____ _____ and _____

_____ .

3b

What can you see here?

e.g. 1. I can see ... and ...

4

Favourite things

e.g. 1. My favourite colour
      is blue.
      2. Our favourite ...
      3. His ...

5

Correct the mistakes:

Susan and (1. his) _____ brother (2. is) _____ from Cambridge. (3. Our) _____
mother and father (4. is) _____ in Cambridge – they (5. has) _____ got (6. an)
____ house in the centre. Susan (7. haven't) _____ got a house – (8. he) _____
(9. are) ____ a student. Susan's brother (10. are) ____ called John and (11. they're)
(12. a) _____ English teacher. John and (13. their) _____ wife (14. has) _____ got
two (15. child) _____ .

6

Write two sentences about each picture.

e.g.

He's a good footballer.
He can play football very well.

He's a bad footballer.
He can play football, but badly.

1. tennis players

2. dancers

3. swimmer

4. cook

5. driver

6. singer

7

Kim's game

Look at this picture for one minute.

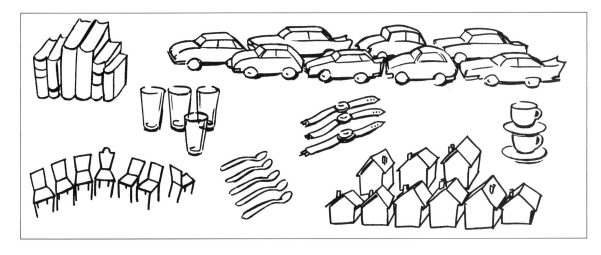

Unit eight – the eighth unit

1a

1:34
11

Ted Johnson lives in Liverpool.
He works in a bank. He goes
to work by bus and he starts
at 9 o'clock. He finishes work
at 5.30. He likes his job.

Caroline Johnson, Ted's wife,
works in a hotel. She starts at
11 o'clock and finishes at
4 o'clock. She goes to work by
car. She likes her job, too.

1b

What's the answer?

Does Mr Johnson live in Liverpool?	Yes, he does. / No, he doesn't.
Does he work in a bank?	Yes, he does. / No, he doesn't.
Does he go to work by bicycle?	Yes, he does. / No, he doesn't.
Does he start at 8 o'clock?	Yes, he does. / No, he doesn't.
Does he finish at 5.30?	Yes, he does. / No, he doesn't.

Does Mrs Johnson live in Liverpool?   *Yes, she does.*

Does she work in a bank?

Does she go to work by bus?

Does she start at 11 o'clock?

Does she finish at 4 o'clock?

1c Ask questions about Mr Johnson.

1. Manchester?   2. in a bank?   3. by bicycle?   4. at 10 o'clock?   5. at 5.30?

Ask questions about Mrs Johnson.

1. Liverpool?   2. in a hotel?   3. by bus?   4. at 11 o'clock?   5. at 4 o'clock?

2a Ask about your partner's mother, father, sister or brother.

e.g. live in Zurich   *Does your mother live in Zurich?*
Yes, she does.   or   *No, she doesn't.*

1. ride a bicycle
2. work in a hotel
3. drink tea
4. drive a car
5. smoke cigars
6. play football
7. make good coffee
8. ski
9. like Coca-Cola
10. put sugar in his / her coffee

2b Now write about your partner's mother, father, sister or brother.

e.g. He / She lives in Zurich.   or   *He / She doesn't live in Zurich.*

1. He / She rides...   or   He / She doesn't ride...
2. works / doesn't work
3. drinks / doesn't drink
4. ...

3a Listen to Christine and Jane. Are these sentences true (T) or false (F)?

1:35

Christine's got a new boyfriend.   *T*

His name's Peter Smith.   _____

He works in an English restaurant.   _____

He works in a hotel.   _____

He works in an Italian restaurant.   _____

He starts work at 9 o'clock.   _____

He starts work at 10 or 4.   _____

He doesn't like his job.   _____

He likes his job.   _____

Christine doesn't like the food in
his restaurant.   _____

3b   Jane has got a new boyfriend, too. What's the first word of these questions?

1. _____ he work in a hotel?   No, he doesn't.

2. _____ he English?   Yes, he is.

3. _____ he speak German?   No, he doesn't.

4. _____ he start work at 9?   No, he doesn't.

5. _____ he like his job?   Yes, he does.

6. _____ he play football on Sundays?   No, he doesn't.

7. _____ he a student?   No, he isn't.

3c   Write about Jane's boyfriend (3b).

e.g. 1. He doesn't work in a hotel.
2. He ...

4a   What day is it today?

It's _____

Monday

Tuesday

Wednesday

Thursday

Friday

Saturday

Sunday

1:36   Listen to Christine on the tape, and write the names Christine (C) or Peter (P) in the boxes.

	Monday	Tuesday	Wednesday	Thursday	Friday	Saturday	Sunday
drive a car	C	C		C	C		
ride a bicycle							
cook dinner							
eat in a restaurant							
learn French							

4b   **Does she ... on Mondays?**   **Does he ... on Fridays?**

e.g. Does Christine drive the car on Wednesdays?   *No, she doesn't.*
Does Peter cook dinner on Thursdays?   *Yes, he does.*

4c

When does Christine ...? When does Peter ...?

e.g. When does Christine ride the bicycle? *She rides it on Saturdays and Sundays.*
When does Peter learn French? *He learns French on Tuesdays.*

4d

Look at 4a. Write about Peter and Christine.

e.g. Peter / car Peter drives the car on Saturdays and Sundays.

1. Peter / dinner
2. Christine / restaurant
3. Christine / French

4. Peter / French
5. Christine / dinner
6. Peter / bicycle

4e

Write three sentences about Peter beginning with *He doesn't ...* , and three sentences about Christine beginning with *She doesn't ...* .

Present simple: he, she

Does	Mr Johnson he she Mrs Johnson	work in a bank? start work at 9? go to work by bus? finish at 5.30?

Yes, he **does.**
No, she **doesn't.**

Mr Johnson	works in a bank. starts work at 9. goes to work by bus. finishes at 5.30.

Mrs Johnson	**doesn't** work in a bank. **doesn't** start work at 9. **doesn't** go to work by bus. **doesn't** finish at 5.30.

Unit nine – the ninth unit

1a

🔘 1:37
💿 12

Tina has got a letter from her boyfriend, Alan, who is in Paris.

Tina: Look, here's a letter from Alan ... he's at school in Paris.

Anna: Oh! How often does he go to school?

Tina: Every day. One week he goes in the mornings and the next week he goes in the afternoons.

Anna: Does he speak English or French in the evenings?

Tina: His family in Paris can't speak English, so he speaks French all the time.

Anna: How often does he write to you?

Tina: Oh! Not often ... once a month.

Anna: But he phones you, doesn't he?

Tina: Oh yes, twice a week.

1b

Alan goes to school every day. He speaks French with his family in Paris because they can only speak French. He writes a letter once a month.

Now write about Susan, George and Maria.

Susan: on Mondays and Thursdays / Italian, Rome / e-mail – 1x – week
George: every morning / German, Heidelberg / letter – 2x – month
Maria: every afternoon / English, London / phone – 2x – week

2a

Alan is at school in Paris. Fill in the missing numbers here:

 1:38

Alan gets up at ___7___ . He eats breakfast at ___7.30___ . He goes to the metro station at _____ . Alan goes to school by metro every day. He arrives at school at _____ when he goes to school in the mornings. He learns French from _____ to _____ . He drinks a cup of coffee at ___10.30___ . At _____ he goes to a restaurant with his friends for lunch. In the afternoons he learns French from _____ to _____ , or he plays tennis. In the evenings, he eats dinner with his French family at _____ .

2b

Ask and answer questions like this about Alan:

e.g. Alan / get up / 7 o'clock

Alan gets up at 7 o'clock, doesn't he?
Yes, that's right.

Alan / eat breakfast / 8

Alan eats breakfast at 8, doesn't he?
No, he doesn't, he eats breakfast at 7.30.

1. Alan / go to the metro station / 8
2. Alan / arrive at school / 9
3. Alan / start the French lessons / 9.30
4. Alan / drink a coffee / 10
5. Alan / have lunch / 12
6. Alan / eat dinner with his French family / 8

3a What's the time?

It's six o'clock.   It's half past six

 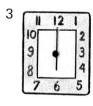  

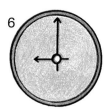  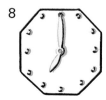 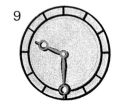 

3b

+ 15 minutes (to the times in 3a)

e.g. 1. It's 8.15 – a quarter past eight.
2. It's 4.45 – a quarter to five.

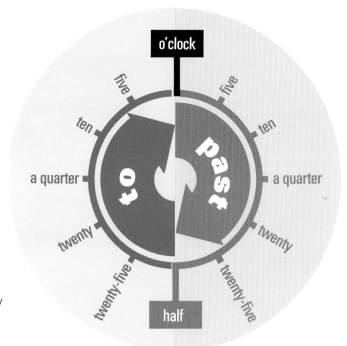

What are these times?
5.20 / 18.35 / 19.05 / 7.50 / 5.55 /
21.40 / 10.10 / 9.25

3c

Make a dialogue.

 1:39
 13

A	B
Excuse me, what's the time, please?	It's …
Excuse me, can you tell me the time, please?	I'm sorry, I don't know.
Excuse me, have you got the time, please?	I'm sorry, I haven't got a watch.

4a

Alan doesn't go to school when he is in England. He works in Manchester. Ask questions about Alan:

e.g. *How often does he go to London?   Once a week.*

How often does he fly to Paris?   Twice a year.

How often does he drink coffee?   Three times a day.

	1x once	2x twice	3x three times	4x four times
day	read the newspaper	drink tea	drink coffee	drive his car
week	go to London	eat in a restaurant	play tennis	see his girlfriend
month	go to the bank	go to the cinema	eat spaghetti	phone his mother
year	play football	fly to Paris	eat Spanish food	write to his brother

4b

He goes to London once a week.   He flies to Paris twice a year.
He drinks coffee three times a day.

1. twice a day
2. play tennis
3. once a year

4. read the newspaper
5. four times a week
6. twice a month

7. go to the bank
8. once a week
9. three times a month

5

How often?

She gets up at 7 every day.	= She **always** gets up at 7.
She reads the newspaper 5 days a week.	= She **usually** reads the newspaper.
She goes to the cinema twice a week.	= She **often** goes to the cinema.
She eats in a restaurant three times a month.	= She **sometimes** eats in a restaurant.
She doesn't drink beer.	= She **never** drinks beer.

Look at the information in exercise 4a. Write about Alan with *always, often, sometimes* or *never.*

e.g. *eat spaghetti*   *He sometimes eats spaghetti.*

1. see his girlfriend
2. go to the cinema
3. play tennis
4. ride a bicycle

5. read the newspaper
6. go to France
7. go skiing
8. eat in a restaurant

6a

🔘 1:40

Listen to Alan and his girlfriend on the phone.
Are these sentences true (T) or false (F)?

Alan ...   T   F

... likes the school.   _____   _____

... always goes to school with his friend John.   _____   _____

... is in a class of twelve students.   _____   _____

... never watches television in the evenings.   _____   _____

... always finishes school at 12.30.   _____   _____

... never eats dinner in a restaurant.   _____   _____

... always does his homework in the evenings.   _____   _____

6b   Four of the sentences in 6a are false. What is correct?

Alan _____ _____ to school with his friend John.

Alan _____ _____ television in the evenings.

Alan _____ _____ school at 12.30.

Alan _____ _____ his homework in the evenings.

7a   Fill in the missing verbs here.

The verbs: PHONE – LEARN – BE – HAVE GOT – FINISH – GO – LIKE – WATCH – DO – WRITE

Maria _____ a student in England. She _____ to a school in the centre of London. She _____ English every day and in the evenings she _____ her homework. She usually _____ her homework in two hours and then she sometimes _____ television. She _____ her mother and father in Italy twice a week. She _____ an e-mail to her boyfriend every day. Maria _____ her school, and she _____ _____ three or four English friends.

7b

Write these words in the correct order to make sentences or questions.

1. goes   She   cinema   Saturdays.   sometimes   the   to   on

2. work?   Where   she   does

3. always   in   bus?   he   Does   newspaper   read   the   the

4. o'clock.   of   at   usually   He   cup   drinks   coffee   a   eleven

5. by   work   goes   She   to   bus.   always

6. with   friends.   never   does   She   her   her   homework

7. write   Does   girlfriend?   his   he   to   often

8. often   Paris?   fly   he   How   does   to

Present simple: he, she

work play drive	He work**s** in a bank. He play**s** football. He drive**s** a car.
fly	He fl**ies** to Paris.
go do	He go**es** at 8 o'clock. He do**es** his homework in the evenings.
finish watch	He finish**es** at 12 o'clock. He watch**es** television in the evenings.

Adverbs of frequency

He She	**always** **usually** **often** **sometimes** **never**	drinks coffee in the mornings. goes to a restaurant for lunch.

Question tags

Where does he live?	He lives in London, **doesn't he?**
Where does she work?	She works in a hotel, **doesn't she?**

Unit ten – the tenth unit

1

🔊 1:41
💿 14

Jane: Can I see that pullover please, the red one?

Lady: Yes, here you are … but it's very expensive.

Jane: How much is it?

Lady: Sixty pounds.

Jane: Sixteen pounds, that isn't very expensive, is it?

Lady: No, not sixteen … sixty … six oh.

Jane: Sixty pounds!! Oh no …

Lady: Yes, it's a bit expensive.

Jane: How much is the blue one?

Lady: That's cheap … it's fifteen pounds.

Jane: Fifteen or fifty?

Lady: Only fifteen.

Jane: Okay … that's better. May I try it on please?

Lady: Yes, of course.

2a

🔊 1:42
💿 15

Listen to these numbers:

10 ten	**33** thirty-three	**60** sixty	**88** eighty-eight
11 eleven	**40** forty	**66** sixty-six	**90** ninety
20 twenty	**44** forty-four	**70** seventy	**99** ninety-nine
22 twenty-two	**50** fifty	**77** seventy-seven	**100** a hundred
30 thirty	**55** fifty-five	**80** eighty	**101** a hundred and one

2b

🔊 1:43

Listen. Which numbers can you hear?   *e.g. 16 or* (60)

a)   13 or 30   c)   15 or 50   e)   17 or 70   g)   19 or 90

b)   14 or 40   d)   16 or 60   f)   18 or 80

3   The alphabet

 1:44
16

a	e	i	m	q	u	y
b	f	j	n	r	v	z
c	g	k	o	s	w	
d	h	l	p	t	x	

4a

These dresses are in Boutique ABC, too.

e.g. Which dress is cheap?   *The English one.*

a) cheap   b) long   c) short   d) expensive   e) big   f) small

A dress from Rome.

cheap

A dress from London.

Look at these two cars.

e.g. Which car is expensive?   *The American one.*

g) expensive   h) old   i) fast   j) cheap   k) slow   l) new

Look at these two men. George is Fred's father.

e.g. Which man is tall? Fred.

m) tall   n) old   o) fat   p) young   q) poor   r) short   s) thin   t) rich

Look at these two hotels.

e.g. Which hotel is modern? The Plaza.

u) modern   v) expensive   w) small   x) old   y) big   z) cheap

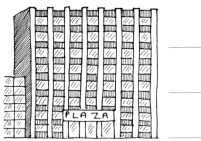

4b

Write two sentences about the dresses, the cars, the men and the hotels.

e.g. The English dress is cheap and the Italian one is expensive.

4c   **What is the opposite of ... ?**

cheap ≠ _____		new ≠ _____		fat ≠ _____
rich ≠ _____		modern ≠ _____		tall ≠ _____
small ≠ _____		young ≠ _____		long ≠ _____
fast ≠ _____				

4d

Write two questions with the word *or* about the dresses, the cars, the men and the hotels. Give your paper to another student. He/she can write the answers.

e.g. Is the Italian dress cheap or expensive?   It's expensive.

5a

How much is ... ? How much are?

Listen to Jane and the lady who works at Boutique ABC.

1:45

5b

Make a dialogue.

A: Can I see that pullover please, the red one?
B: Yes, here you are.
A: How much is it?
B: £60.
A: £60! ... oh, that's very expensive.

skirt	(£23.50, £29.95)
dress	(£39.95, £200)
shoes	(£21, £43)

cheap
not too expensive
too expensive
a bit expensive

6

Find out the missing information about the lady who works at Boutique ABC.

Your teacher has got the answers, but your teacher only answers correct questions!

Mrs (1) _____ Jones works at Boutique ABC. This modern boutique is in the (2) _____ _____ _____ . Mrs Jones lives (3) _____ _____ from the boutique. She gets up at (4) _____ every morning and always eats (5) _____ for breakfast and she drinks (6) _____ too. She goes to the shop at (7) _____ and she finishes at (8) _____ in the evenings. She works at the shop (9) _____ days a week. She (10) likes / doesn't like her job very much.

Here are the first words of the questions: (1) What is ... (2) Where ... (3) Where does ... (4) What time does ... (5) What ... (6) What ... (7) What time ... (8) What time ... (9) How many ... (10) Does ...

Adjectives

The American car is **expensive**.	It's an **expensive** car.
Those cars are **expensive**.	They're **expensive** cars.
The Plaza hotel is **modern**.	It's a **modern** hotel.
Those hotels are **modern**.	They're **modern** hotels.

Question word: which | **One / ones**

Which pullover does he want?	The red one.
Which is your book?	The English one.
Which shoes does she like?	The blue ones.
Which houses are cheap?	The old ones.

A. DENIM JACKET 39.99
STONEWASHED

B. JEANS 19.99

AMERICANO brand

C. SHIRT 15.99
D. SKIRT 18.99

A DENIM JACKET.
Loose style blouson in
stonewashed cotton
denim with contrast
acrylic fur trim and
brushed cotton lining.
Length: 27ins.
Washable. Blue.
Sizes: 10/12. 14/16.
BE 52 53   £39.99
          20wks £2.00
          38wks £1.06

B JEANS.
Western styling in
stonewashed cotton
denim. To fit inside leg:
29ins. Washable.
Sizes: 10, 12, 14, 16.
BE 26 64 Blue
BE 26 65 Black
£19.99   20wks £1.00

C CHECK SHIRT.
Loose fitter in brushed
cotton. Washable.
Sizes: 10/12, 14/16.
BE 05 50 Red
BE 05 51 Yellow
£15.99   20wks 80p

D SKIRT.
Shorter length style
with zip detail. In
the new 'off the
wall' stonewashed
heavyweight twill.
Length: 21ins.
Washable. Cotton. Grey.
Sizes: 10, 12, 14.
BE 15 96   £18.99
          20wks 95p

E. JACKET 31.95
F. JEANS 25.99

EASY.

B. BLUE STONEWASH

A. SWEATER 17.99

SHIRTS AND SWEATERS
THAT STAND OUT FROM THE
CROWD, HAND PICKED
ESPECIALLY FOR YOU

B. SWEATER 16.99

G. TOP 17.99
H. SKIRT 17.99

E JACKET.
By Easy. Wide styling
in the new 'off the
wall' stonewashed
heavyweight twill.
Washable. Cotton. Grey.
Sizes: 8/10, 12/14.
BE 52 67   £31.95
          20wks £1.60

F JEANS.
By Easy. Western style.
Tight-fitters taper to
12ins. ankles. In 'off
the wall' stonewashed
heavyweight twill.
Washable. Cotton. Grey.
Sizes: 8, 10, 12, 14.
BE 26 37   £25.99
          20wks £1.30

G BUTTONED TOP.
Grandad style long-liner
with shoulder pads. In
new marl jersey.
Washable. Acrylic. Grey.
Sizes: 10/12, 14/16.
BE 38 04   £17.99
          20wks 90p

For belt see page 14

H SKIRT.
Full swirly style with
elasticated waist. In new
marl jersey. Length:
32ins. Washable.
Acrylic. Grey.
Sizes: 10/12, 14/16.
BE 15 85   £17.99
          20wks 90p

A SWEATER.
In a jacquard design with
crew neck. Acrylic. Grey.
Order size: S, M, L.
ME 86 58
£17.99   20wks 90p

B SWEATER.
With polo collar and 3 button
fastening placket. Acrylic.
Jade/Black.
Order size: S, M, L.
ME 86 57 £16.99 20wks 85p

27

For shoes see page 14

Unit eleven – the eleventh unit

1 A boy and a girl are at the disco.

2:1
18

Boy: Hello, what's your name?
Girl: Suzie.
Boy: Do you come here often?
Girl: Yes, I do – every Friday evening.
Boy: Do you live near here then?
Girl: Yes, I do.
Boy: Do you like the music here?
Girl: Yes, I do.
Boy: Do you work near here?
Girl: No, I don't. Can I ask you a question?
Boy: Yes, of course.
Girl: Do you always ask so many questions?

2a Write *'Yes, I do'* or *'No, I don't'* as the answer to these questions:

1. Do you go to a disco every Friday evening? _____

2. Do you live near your school? _____

3. Do you drink coffee in the mornings? _____

4. Do you come to school by bus? _____

5. Do you start school at 9 o'clock? _____

6. Do you play football with your friends? _____

7. Do you like fish? _____

8. Do you watch television in the evenings? _____

2b Now ask questions 1–8 to your partner.

3a

2:2

Listen to the six conversations on the tape. Match the conversations to these pictures:

3b

2:2

Listen again. How many questions with *do you* can you hear in the conversations?

1. ____   2. ____   3. ____   4. ____   5. ____   6. ____

4a

This is Frank. He's from California. He works at the Disco Futura. He's the disc jockey.
Write questions for Frank, beginning with *Do you … ?*

*e.g. Ask Frank if he works in the evenings.
Do you work in the evenings, Frank?*

Ask Frank if he

a) likes disco music
b) drinks beer at the disco
c) works 7 evenings a week
d) smokes
e) sometimes goes to a disco to dance
f) lives with his mother
g) likes his job
h) plays a musical instrument

4b   Your teacher is Frank, the disc jockey. Ask your questions.

5a

Ask possible questions. Answer *Yes, ...* or *No, ...*

Do	you		football?
		like	French?
			in a bank?
		play	near this school?
			spaghetti?
		work	tennis?
Does	your brother		coffee?
	your sister	speak	a musical instrument?
	your mother		in an office?
	your father	live	pop music?
			Italian?
			in Zurich?

5b   What are the answers?

Do you go to the Disco Futura?	Yes, I do. / No, I don't.
Does your teacher like pop music?	Yes, _____ does. / No, _____ doesn't.
Do you and your friends learn English on Mondays?	Yes, we do. / No, we don't.
Do teachers work on Sundays?	Yes, they do. / No, they don't.
Do you like discos?	Yes, I do. / No, I don't.
Do you and your family live near your school?	Yes, we do. / No, we don't.

Do you like pop music?   _____

Does your teacher smoke?   _____

Do you and your friends learn Spanish at school?   _____

Do people in London live in tents?   _____

6

Write these sentences correctly ... and find an answer.

1. me?   like   you   Do

2. get up?   time   you   What   do

3. go   you   to the cinema?   do   How often

4. the   you   dinner?   Do   cook

5. does   he   work?   Where

6. When   lunch?   have   you   do

7. by bicycle?   Why   he   to the office   does   go

8. pop music?   Do   your friends   like   you   and

He hasn't got a job
    At half past six.
Yes, but not on Fridays!
Yes, I do!
Once a week.
    At 12 o'clock.   Yes, we do!
Because he hasn't got a car.

7a   A letter from Claire

Sea View,
Victoria Road,
Stanton-Upon-Sea
England ST7 3YJ
Friday lunchtime.

Dear...,

Thank you for your letter... your English is good!
I can't write or speak a word of German. Oh yes!! I can!
KINDERGARTEN - that word is in English, too. Tell me about your
friends at school. My best friend is called Pat.
What are your friends called? Pat doesn't live
in the next house to me, but she lives in the
next street, at number 73. Where does your best friend live?

Do you learn English at primary school or at
secondary school? We start French at primary school, and then
at secondary school we can learn Italian or German (or
sometimes Spanish). I'm not very good at French. Can
you speak French? Do your mother and father or your
brother or sister speak English, too?

Today is Friday... it's Disco Futura day... hurray,
hurray. Please write to me ~~today~~ soon.

← sorry... horrible
mess!!

Love from,

Claire

7b   Write a short letter to Claire. You can find help with words in her letter.

7c Find the correct endings for these questions:

1. Claire's English, *isn't she* ?

2. Claire's got a friend called Pat, _____ ?

3. Pat lives in the next street, _____ ?

4. Pat and her friends learn French at school, _____ ?

5. Kindergarten is an English word too, _____ ?

6. You learn French too, _____ ?

don't you?   doesn't she?   isn't she?
don't they?   hasn't she?   isn't it?

8 Make a dialogue.

 2:3
 19

A: How often do you go to the disco?

B: Once a week.

A: Why do you go there?

B: Because I like the music they have.

A: When do you go there?

B: Every Friday evening.

do	you	I		disco
	you + Suzie	we	like	cinema
	Paul	he		restaurant
does	Caroline	she	likes	snack bar
	Ann + Peter	they		

music
films
food
coffee

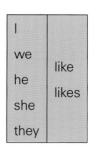

Present simple: I, you, we, they

Do	you you and Pat they	work here?

Does	John Susan	go to the disco?

Yes,	I we they	**do.**

No,	I we they	**don't.**

Yes,	he she	**does.**

No,	he she	**doesn't.**

Question words: where, what, when

Where do you live? Where does he work? What does she like? When do you start? What do they read?	I live in London. He works in a school. She likes spaghetti. We start at 8 o'clock. They read newspapers.	I don't live in Manchester. He doesn't work in an office. She doesn't like beer. We don't start at 7 o'clock. They don't read books.

Unit twelve – the twelfth unit

1a   Judy is in a coffee bar. She's alone ...

 2:4
 20

Tom: Hello, Judy, can I sit here?
Judy: Yes, Tom ... of course, sit down.
Tom: I must have a cup of coffee –
       would you like one, too?
Judy: No, thanks very much ...
       I don't like coffee.
Tom: How about a cup of tea,
       then?
Judy: No, thanks ... I know, I'd like
       an orange juice, please.
Tom: Fine ... Waiter! We'd like one
       glass of orange juice and one
       coffee, please.

1b   Match these words:

a glass of _____

a bottle of _____

a cup of   _____

a cup of   _____

a pot of   _____

a pot of   _____

a cup of   _____

a glass of _____

hot chocolate
tea
coffee
mineral water
milk
orange juice

1c   Make dialogues like the one between Tom and Judy in 1a, but with different drinks. Here are
         some drinks to choose from:

coffee   tea   orange juice   milk   mineral   hot
                                                                 water   chocolate

1d

Make a dialogue.

A: Do you like milk?

B: No, I don't.

> *words in exercise 1b*
> apples
> eggs
> Coca-Cola
> oranges

A: Do you like milk?

B: Yes, I do.

A: Would you like a glass of milk now?

B: No, thanks very much … not now.
   (**or** Yes, please!)

2

An offer or a question?

e.g. Would you like a cup of tea?   (an offer)
    Yes, please. or *No, thanks very much.*

Would you like to have this book?   (an offer)
Yes, please. or *No, thank you.*

Would you like to live in America?   (a question)
Yes, I would. or *No, I wouldn't.*

Ask these questions:

- a cup of tea
- a hamburger
- to live in America
- to come to the cinema
- Coca-Cola
- sandwich
- to learn Spanish
- to have a car
- a cigar
- a glass of orange juice
- to go to Africa
- a beer

- to be a pop singer
- to come swimming at 4
- to have more brothers or
  sisters
- an apple
- a cup of coffee
- to learn to dance
- a glass of wine
- to live in a big house
- a cigarette
- an orange
- a mineral water

Possible answers:

> Yes, please.
>
> No, thanks very much.
>
> No, thank you.
>
> Yes, I would.
>
> No, I wouldn't.

3a

 2:5

Listen to the conversations in a pizzeria. Write the missing numbers on the waiter's orders.

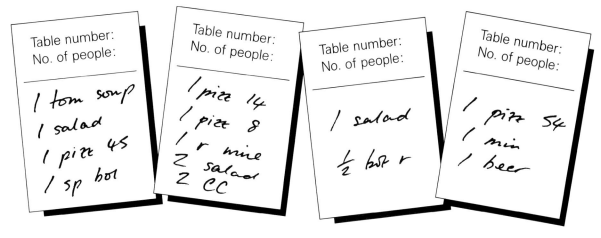

3b　Listen to the first dialogue again and fill in the missing words.

2:6　Waiter:　Good _____ , sir. What _____ you _____ to order?

Man:　Well, I'd _____ something _____ – is it possible _____ order just a salad _____ that's all?

Waiter:　Certainly, sir – and _____ _____ _____ anything to _____ ?

Man:　Yes – bring me a _____ _____ of your house wine – _____ _____ .

4a　**The birthday cake**

2:7　Listen to Tom and Judy – they are still in the coffee bar. Are the sentences here true (T) or false (F)?

	T	F
It's Judy's birthday soon.	_____	_____
Susan's birthday is next week.	_____	_____
Susan would like a pop music cassette.	_____	_____
Susan likes pop music.	_____	_____
Tom thinks a ticket to a concert is a good idea.	_____	_____
Tom's birthday is in December.	_____	_____
Judy's birthday is on 7th April.	_____	_____
Judy says Susan wouldn't like a birthday cake.	_____	_____

4b　Complete the following list. You can find the words *first* etc. at the beginning of every unit. Here are the months of the year:

August, May, December, January, June, October, February, November, March, September, April, July

The *first* month is *January* .　The _____ month is _____ .

The _____ month is _____ .　The _____ month is _____ .

The _____ month is _____ .　The _____ month is _____ .

The _____ month is _____ .　The _____ month is _____ .

The _____ month is _____ .　The _____ month is _____ .

The _____ month is _____ .　The _____ month is _____ .

2:8　Now listen to the correct answers.

4c   Listen to the dialogue between Tom and Judy again.

2:9   When is Susan's birthday?   It's on *12th November.*

When is Tom's birthday?   It's on _____

When is your birthday?   It's on _____

When is your teacher's birthday?   It's on _____

4d   Say the following sentences.

You write *Susan's birthday is on 12th November* but you say *Susan's birthday is on the 12th of November.*

a) George   / 3.2   c) Caroline   / 1.5   e) Fred   / 2.3
b) Anna   / 5.7   d) Christine / 8.1   f) Peter   / 9.6

Would like

I You He/she We You They	**'d like**	a car. an apple. to live in Italy.

Would you **like**	a cup of tea? an orange juice?

	Yes, please.
No,	thank you. thanks very much.

Would	I you he/she we you they	**like**	to go to the concert? to see that film?

Yes,	I you he/she	**would.**
No,	we you they	**wouldn't.**

Unit thirteen – the thirteenth unit

1a

Dear Paul & Karin,
This place is very nice &
interesting, too. There's a
swimming pool in our hotel
& there are 6 tennis courts.
We play tennis every day...
the weather is good. Is it
cold at home? There's a
disco here, too – but it's
always too crowded and too
smoky. There are 2 good
restaurants, too .. and we
always eat too much!!
We've got one more week
here.   Love
          Fred & Tanya

Paul & Karin Davies
33 The Drive
LONDON NH3 2JE
ENGLAND

Where are Fred and Tanya? Are they at Buntines Hotel in Rabat, in Algiers or in Tunis?

BUNTINES IN RABAT
•
Buntines for you!

★ swimming pool
★ 6 tennis courts
★ bar
★ 3 restaurants
★ disco
★ hotel bus

BUNTINES
IN THE
SUNSHINE

BUNTINES IN ALGIERS
•
Buntines for you!

★ swimming pool
★ 4 tennis courts
★ bar
★ 2 restaurants
★ disco
★ video club

BUNTINES
IN THE
SUNSHINE

BUNTINES IN TUNIS
•
Buntines for you!

★ swimming pool
★ 6 tennis courts
★ bar
★ 2 restaurants
★ disco
★ mini golf

BUNTINES
IN THE
SUNSHINE

Fred and Tanya are at Buntines Hotel in _____ .

At this Buntines holiday hotel there's a _____ _____ , a _____ , a _____

and a _____ _____ . There are six _____ _____ and two

_____ .

1b   Is there a ... ?   Are there two ... ?

e.g. Is there a swimming pool at Buntines in Rabat?   *Yes, there is.*
Are there two swimming pools at Buntines in Rabat?   *No, there's only one.*
Is there a video club at Buntines in Rabat?   *No, there isn't.*

a) bar / Buntines in Algiers
b) mini golf / Buntines in Rabat
c) hotel bus / Buntines in Tunis
d) disco / Buntines in Algiers

e) swimming pool / Buntines in Tunis
f) hotel bus / Buntines in Rabat
g) video club / Buntines in Tunis
h) video club / Buntines in Algiers

1c   Are there any ... ?   How many ... are there?

e.g. Are there any tennis courts at Buntines in Rabat?   *Yes, there are.*
How many tennis courts are there?   *There are six.*
Are there six tennis courts at Buntines in Algiers, too? *No, there aren't.*

a) restaurants / Buntines in Tunis
b) tennis courts / Buntines in Algiers
c) tennis courts / Buntines in Tunis

d) restaurants / Buntines in Rabat
e) restaurants / Buntines in Algiers

1d

2:10

Buntines have got four new hotels for next summer. Listen to the telephone conversation about these new hotels and fill in the information here.

	rooms	lift	restaurant	bar	disco	video/TV room	swimming pool	tennis courts	mini golf	hotel bus
Valencia	80	✗	1							
Palermo		✓								
Corfu										
St. Tropez										

1e

You are at one of these Buntines hotels. Write a postcard to your friends. Begin like this:

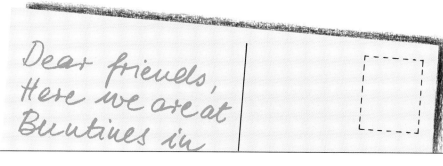

Dear friends,
Here we are at
Buntines in

2a

My name's Tanya. Fred and I are at Buntines Hotel in Tunis. We like this hotel ... we've got a very nice room with a big window and a view of the sea. Here's a picture of our room ...

Match the letters in the picture with these words:

_____ alarm clock	_____ chair	_____ picture
_____ ashtray	_____ cupboard	_____ plant
_____ balcony	_____ curtain	_____ radio
_____ bed	_____ drawer	_____ telephone
_____ bedside table	_____ lamp	_____ television
_____ carpet	_____ mirror	_____ waste paper basket

2b   Is there a ... in your bedroom?

e.g. Is there a chair in your bedroom?   *Yes, there is.*
                                                  No, there isn't.

   How many chairs are there in your bedroom?   *There's only one.*
                                                  There are two (or three, or ...)

3a   Tunis is too hot for me, and Buntines Hotel is too expensive for me ...

... but not for Tanya and Fred!

Why don't Tanya and Fred like the disco at Buntines Hotel in Tunis?

Because it's too _____ and too _____ .

3b   Finish these sentences using the word *too:*

a) Susan, who has got £10 in the bank, wants to have a holiday at Buntines Hotel. She can't because *she's too poor.*

b) Carol would like to stay at the Plaza Hotel, but it's £200 a night. She can't stay there because *it's too...*

c) George, who is 65 years old, wants to be a pilot. He can't because ...

d) Peter, who is 1 metre 50 tall, wants to be a basketball player. He can't ...

e) The two children, who are 7 and 9 years old, want to go to the disco. They ...

f) Paul wants to drink his coffee, which is 100 °C at the moment. He ...

g) Suzie, who types 10 words a minute, wants to be the manager's secretary. She ...

WARNING!
There are some new words in this exercise, some words that you don't know – look in the word list if you don't understand.

4a   All these people would like to have a job at Buntines Hotel in Tunis. Are they good for the jobs they want or not? Find an ending for the sentences in the boxes.

a) Suzie wants to be the manager's secretary but she can only type 10 words per minute. She *isn't* a good person for the job because *she types very slowly* .

b) Peter wants to be the receptionist but his French isn't good. He _____ a good receptionist because _____ _____ _____ _____ _____ .

c) Caroline wants to work in the restaurant which is always very crowded. She's always very quick, never slow. She _____ right for the job because _____ _____ _____ _____ .

d) Nina wants to be the telephonist. People can always understand her on the phone. She _____ the right person for the job because _____ _____ _____ _____ .

e) George wants to be the driver but he doesn't concentrate and always looks at attractive girls in the street. He _____ good for the job because _____ _____ _____ _____ .

f) Patrick wants to be the receptionist. His French is excellent. He _____ the man for the job because _____ _____ _____ _____ _____ .

g) Amanda wants to be the manager's secretary. She never makes mistakes in her work. She _____ a very good secretary because _____ _____ _____ _____ .

h) Anna wants to be the singer. It's impossible to understand the words when she sings. She _____ right for the job because _____ _____ _____ _____ .

she speaks very clearly.

he drives very carelessly.

he speaks French very well.

she types very slowly.

she works very carefully.

she sings very unclearly.

he speaks French very badly.

she works very quickly.

4b

Ask questions about the people who want jobs at Buntines Hotel in Tunis.

e.g. slowly or quickly *Does Suzie type slowly or quickly?* *She types slowly.*
  Does Caroline work slowly or quickly? *She works quickly.*

a) well or badly   b) clearly or unclearly   c) carefully or carelessly

There is / there are

There**'s (is)**	a lift a swimming pool a disco	in this hotel.

There **are**	6 tennis courts 2 restaurants 3 bars	in this hotel.

Is there **a** video club in this hotel?	Yes, there **is.**
	No, there **isn't.**

Are there **any** conference rooms in this hotel?	Yes, there **are.**
	No, there **aren't.**

Adverbs

She's a **good** tennis player.	She plays tennis **well.**
He's a **bad** singer.	He sings **badly.**
She's a **slow** typist.	She types **slowly.**
He's a **quick** worker.	He works **quickly.**
She's a **clear** speaker.	She speaks **clearly.**
He's a **careless** driver.	He drives **carelessly.**
She's a **careful** writer.	She writes **carefully.**

Unit fourteen – the fourteenth unit

1

Do you remember Mr and Mrs Johnson in Unit 8?
Look at page 38 again.
Write ten sentences about Mr and Mrs Johnson with the words in these boxes.

Mr Johnson	goes to work	their jobs. by bus.
Mrs Johnson	live	at 5.30. at 11 o'clock. in a bank.
Mr and Mrs Johnson	finishes work	at 9. by car. in Liverpool.
	like	at 4 o'clock. in a hotel.
	starts work	
	works	

2a

Which verb goes with these words? You can find all the verbs here (→ ↓ ↘):

e.g. *Work* in a bank

	a glass of milk
	'thank you' to the waiter
	a letter to a friend
	a coffee from the waiter
	at 6 in the morning
	to the bank by bus
	dinner for a friend
	in a house in Manchester
	French at school
	work at 9 o'clock
	work at 5 o'clock

	1	2	3	4	5	6	7	8	9	10
a	G	E	T	U	P	U	Q	E	L	G
b	T	Q	L	P	G	V	J	C	I	R
c	C	B	O	E	F	W	D	D	V	Y
d	E	D	Y	N	A	O	R	D	E	R
e	Z	S	G	B	N	R	I	I	S	I
f	A	J	C	O	O	K	N	P	T	X
g	E	B	F	V	K	O	K	Z	A	E
h	F	I	N	I	S	H	R	H	R	H
i	K	C	W	M	A	L	S	F	T	U
j	A	L	I	M	Y	A	T	X	W	D

2b   Have you and your partner got the same answers?

A: Have you got the verb which goes with 'in a bank'?
B: Yes, it's 'work' … from 6c to 6f. Have you got it too?
A: …

3   Make these sentences into questions by writing two words at the end:

e.g. She's an English teacher, *isn't she* ?

1. He works in a bank, *d*_____ ?
2. They're in London today, *a*_____ ?
3. You like pop music, *d*_____ ?
4. She'd like to go to Paris, *w*_____ ?
5. He can speak English, *c*_____ ?
6. They've got two sons, *h*_____ ?
7. London is very big, *i*_____ ?
8. The children learn French, *d*_____ ?

4a   **The months of the year and the days of the week.**

R E B T O C O	*October*	Y M A	
M R H C A		S Y U A D N	
D I Y A R F		U A S T E Y D	
N J Y A A U R		S U G A T U	
D D E E S Y W N A		E J N U	
L U Y J		U S T Y H D R A	
Y A T S D R U A		V R B E E O N M	
B M R E D C E E		R R Y F A E U B	
N M Y D O A		I L A R P	
E E E P B S T R M			

4b   Fill in the information here … you can only write numbers – NO WORDS!

2:11   e.g. John's interview is at *11.15* on *12.4.* .

1. The concert starts at _____ on _____ .
2. The train to Rome is at _____ on _____ .
3. Tanya's interview is at _____ on _____ .
4. The first lesson is at _____ on _____ .
5. The football starts at _____ on _____ .
6. The opera is at _____ on _____ .

5a   Correct the mistakes:

Mr Davison (1. work) _____ in a bank, and (2. her) _____ job's very interesting. He

(3. have) _____ got two (4. child) _____ and they (5. goes) ____ to school

in Bristol. His (6. husband) _____ is (7. an) ___ teacher. She (8. teach)_____

music. They live in a house in Bristol, but they (9. doesn't) _____ like Bristol, they'd

(10. likes) _____ to live in London. (11. My) _____ house in Bristol is (12. to)

_____ small, there (13. is) _____ only two bedrooms. Mr Davison sometimes

(14. ask) _____ his wife "How many (15. bedroom) _____ (16. does) ____

we want?" And (17. he) _____ always says "I (18. doesn't) _____ know – three

or (19. for) _____ – what (20. you think) _____ _____ _____ ?" But Mr

Davison doesn't know.

5b   Write questions about the Davison family. You can see the answers here:

e.g. In a bank.   Where does Mr Davison work?

The first word of every question is in the box.

a) Two (a boy and a girl).
b) In Bristol.
c) Yes, she is.
d) Music.
e) No, they don't.
f) Only two.

5c   Write about Mr Davison or Mrs Davison.

e.g. Mr Davison usually eats breakfast at 7.30.

breakfast / 7.30 (usually)

work / 8.30 (always)

bank

coffee / mornings
(sometimes)

lunch / 12 / restaurant
(usually)

tea / 3 (always)

work / 5 o'clock (always)

breakfast / 8 (sometimes)

work / 9 (always)

music

coffee / 10.30 (usually)

lunch / 12.30 snack bar
(sometimes)

work / afternoons (never)

dinner for Mr Davison (usually)

6   Use the word in brackets ( ) in the correct form in the sentences.

e.g. (careless)   He's a *careless* driver. He drives *carelessly* .

1. (good)   She sings _____ . She's a _____ singer.

2. (clear)   He speaks _____ . He's a _____ speaker.

3. (bad)   He's a _____ driver. He drives _____ .

4. (quick)   She reads _____ . She's a _____ reader.

5. (careful)   They are _____ workers. They work _____ .

6. (slow)   She's a _____ typist. She types _____ .

7a   Write these words in the correct order to make questions.

a) you   would   to   America   in   live   like

_____ ?

b) like   food   you   do   Spanish

_____ ?

c) tea   a   of   cup   like   you   coffee   or   would   a

_____ ?

d) you   eat   to   what   like   would

_____ ?

e) pop   like   or   do   opera   music   you

_____ ?

7b   Now ask a partner these questions.

8   You want to find a friend for a holiday. You want a person who:

- likes pop music
- doesn't smoke
- has got a car
- doesn't drink beer
- speaks French
- isn't more than 20 years old
- would like to go camping
- can go on holiday in July

What questions do you want to ask?

e.g. Do you like pop music?

Unit fifteen – the fifteenth unit

1a This is Joe Jones from Jacksville. Joe is poor and he's unhappy, too. He hasn't got a job and he hasn't got a rich uncle, either. Joe's got a wife and three children, but no money. He must do something, but he doesn't know what. His friends all think they know what he can do!

1b Listen to what his friends say and write in the verbs here:

2:18

Find
Learn
Ask
Try
Look
Sell
Play
Rob
Go
Work

1. _____ cards in Las Vegas, Joe.

2. _____ to New York, Joe.

3. _____ a rich woman, Joe.

4. _____ for your father, Joe.

5. _____ for a job, Joe.

6. _____ to print money, Joe.

7. _____ your car, Joe.

8. _____ a friend for $1,000, Joe.

9. _____ the lottery, Joe.

10. _____ a bank, Joe.

1c But Joe doesn't think these ideas are very good. Which answer does he give to which friend?

I can't do that – they're all too poor.

I can't do that – there's always a better man.

I can't do that – I don't want a problem with the police.

I can't do that – the ticket's too expensive.

I can't do that – I haven't got one.

I can't do that – I never win.

I can't do that – he lives in Alaska.

I can't do that – I've got a wife and three children.

1d

Write ten sentences about Joe Jones – the information is in 1b and 1c.
Here's the first sentence:

1. He can't play cards in Las Vegas because he never wins.
2. ...

2

Here is a story about another Mr Jones, this time it's Dale Jones. What differences between Dale's life and Joe's life can you hear?

2:19

3a

Joe Jones is in a restaurant in Jacksville with a friend. Joe is very unhappy because he's poor. Here is their conversation. Joe starts – put his friend's sentences in the correct order.

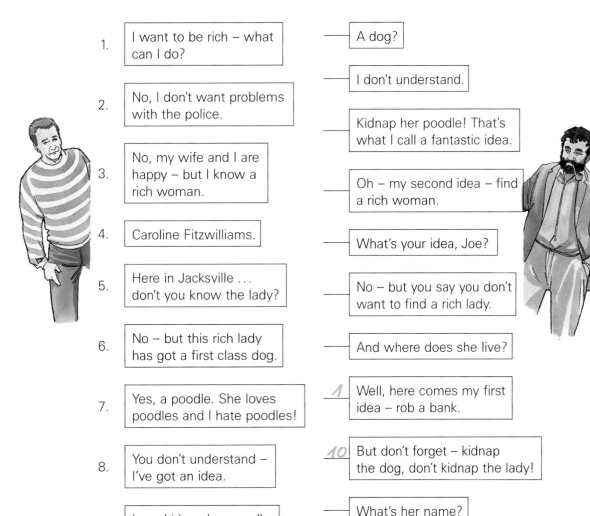

1. I want to be rich – what can I do?

2. No, I don't want problems with the police.

3. No, my wife and I are happy – but I know a rich woman.

4. Caroline Fitzwilliams.

5. Here in Jacksville ... don't you know the lady?

6. No – but this rich lady has got a first class dog.

7. Yes, a poodle. She loves poodles and I hate poodles!

8. You don't understand – I've got an idea.

9. I can kidnap her poodle and ask for $5,000.

10. Yes – a fantastic idea.

A dog?

I don't understand.

Kidnap her poodle! That's what I call a fantastic idea.

Oh – my second idea – find a rich woman.

What's your idea, Joe?

No – but you say you don't want to find a rich lady.

And where does she live?

1 Well, here comes my first idea – rob a bank.

10 But don't forget – kidnap the dog, don't kidnap the lady!

What's her name?

3b

Joe and his friend always have the same ideas and do the same things. Write about Joe's friend.

e.g. Joe is in a restaurant. *His friend is in a restaurant,* **too.**
    Joe isn't rich.   *His friend isn't rich,* **either.**

1. Joe lives in Jacksville.
2. Joe doesn't like poodles.
3. Joe hasn't got a car.
4. Joe is a good man.

5. Joe knows a rich lady.
6. Joe is married.
7. Joe isn't rich.
8. Joe doesn't want problems.

4a   **Who can help Joe?**

Which of these words go together?

she you they I he we you

J – me _____ _____

_____ _____

_____

him you us them her you me

4b   Write sentences like this one:

e.g. Dad, please buy us a tent.

He'd like to buy them a tent, but he can't.

a) Joe, please give me a gold ring.

b) Joe, can you buy me a drink?

c) Joe, can you invite me to dinner?

d) Dad, can you give us $100 please?

e) Joe, can you buy me a new dress?

f) Dad, please give us some money for next Saturday.

5   Joe has got the rich lady's poodle. Now he wants to write a letter to the lady to ask for money. He has got the words from the newspaper – write the letter for him.

to   the   alone   MIDNIGHT   at

ON   police

THE $5,000   Happy Sam's

contact

NEWSPAPER   phone   Hamburger Palace   SATURDAY

Bring _____

DON'T _____

Don't _____

COME _____

6   The end of the story of Joe Jones of Jacksville and the rich lady's poodle!

 2:20

7   Which do you think is correct?

e.g. Joe to the rich lady: ~~Phone~~
                                 (Don't phone) the police.

Teacher to a student:

Open
Don't open   your book at page three.

Listen
Don't listen   to the tape, ready?

Bring
Don't bring   your book on Friday, there's no lesson.

Mother to her little boy:

_____ worms, they're not good for you. (eat)

_____ to bed now, it's nine o'clock!   (go)

_____ it's okay ... I'm here.   (cry)

Doctor to a man:

_____ Mr Smith.

_____ swimming twice a week, Mr Smith.

_____ and see me on Monday at 11.

come
     smoke
go

Imperatives

Go to the bank. **Ask** for $ 5,000. **Bring** the money at midnight.

Don't come with a friend. **Don't phone** the police. **Don't contact** the newspaper.

Object pronouns

subject		possessive		object
I You He She We You They	would like to take	my your his her our your their	money with	me. you. him. her. us. you. them.

Too / either

+	+
I like poodles. He lives in Jacksville.	She likes poodles, **too.** They live in Jacksville, **too.**
—	**—**
He doesn't work here. We haven't got a car.	You don't work here, **either.** They haven't got a car, **either.**

Unit sixteen – the sixteenth unit

1a Jack and his friend Thomas (Tom for short) are students. They aren't very rich and they haven't got cars. A lot of students ride bicycles, but Jack and Tom have both got new mopeds. Now they must both get a licence for the mopeds. They mustn't ride the mopeds without a licence!

Info 2009:
Jack und Thomas are still good friends now – they still live in Oxford and they're 37 years old. They drive family cars now.

1b

◉ 2:21

Jack and Tom are in the Town Hall now. They're in the driving licence office. Fill in the details about Jack and Tom here:

DRIVING LICENCE APPLICATION FORM
Surname:
First name(s):
Address:
Telephone:
Date of birth:
Type of vehicle: ☐ car ☐ motorbike ☐ moped
Engine capacity: ccs
Colour:
Make:
Vehicle number:
Date:
Signature:
FORM 35976/L

DRIVING LICENCE APPLICATION FORM
Surname:
First name(s):
Address:
Telephone:
Date of birth:
Type of vehicle: ☐ car ☐ motorbike ☐ moped
Engine capacity: ccs
Colour:
Make:
Vehicle number:
Date:
Signature:
FORM 35976/L

2a

Before they get a licence, Jack and Tom must also learn the road signs. Do you know them? Match the road signs on the left, with a sentence from the boxes on the right.

e.g. 1. You must go straight on here.

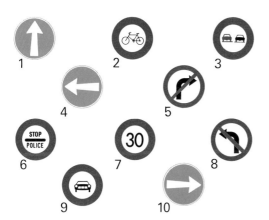

You	must	overtake here.
		turn right here.
		turn left here.
		ride a bicycle here.
		go over 30 here.
	mustn't	stop here.
		drive a car here.
		go straight on here.

2b

Test your partner on the road signs. Your partner can look at the signs, but mustn't look at the sentences in the boxes!

3

Jack and Tom want to go camping in Scotland. They don't want to take too many things, but there are some things that they must take. They must take sleeping bags, for example, but they don't have to take campbeds because they can sleep on the ground. They must take some money too, but they don't have to take Scottish pounds because you can spend English pounds in Scotland.

Which of these things do you think they must take on their trip? Which things aren't necessary?

e.g. 1. They must take sleeping bags.
2. They don't have to take campbeds.

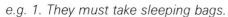
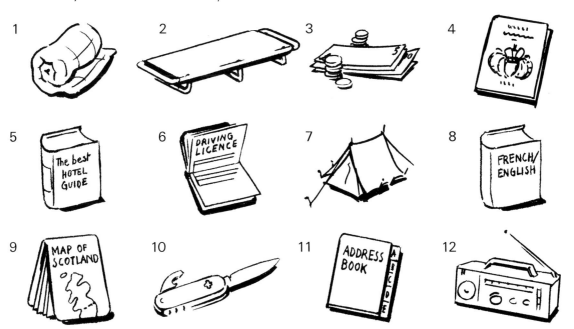

4   Jack and Tom are at a campsite near Loch Ness. They want to eat in the snack bar because it's cheap there. There's a list of rules at the campsite:

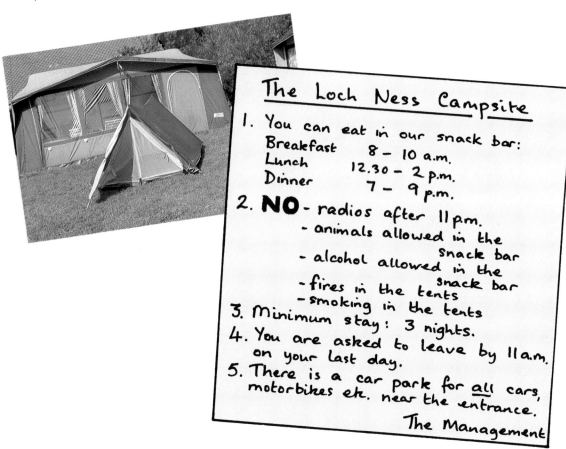

The Loch Ness Campsite

1. You can eat in our snack bar:
   Breakfast   8 – 10 a.m.
   Lunch   12.30 – 2 p.m.
   Dinner   7 – 9 p.m.
2. **NO** - radios after 11 p.m.
   - animals allowed in the snack bar
   - alcohol allowed in the snack bar
   - fires in the tents
   - smoking in the tents
3. Minimum stay: 3 nights.
4. You are asked to leave by 11 a.m. on your last day.
5. There is a car park for all cars, motorbikes etc. near the entrance.

The Management

Write sentences with *must, mustn't* or *don't have to* about Jack and Tom.

e.g. have breakfast before 10   *They must have breakfast before 10.*
     have breakfast at 8   *They don't have to have breakfast at 8.*
     take a dog into the snack bar   *They mustn't take a dog into the snack bar.*

1. have lunch before 2   6. stay for a minimum of 3 nights

2. have lunch at 1   7. stay for 4 nights

3. leave by 11 o'clock on the last day 8. park the mopeds next to the tents

4. listen to radios at 2 in the morning 9. have dinner at 8 o'clock

5. drink beer in the snack bar   10. make a fire in the tent

5   Write *must* or *mustn't* in these sentences. They are rules for your class!

We _____ speak English.   We _____ play cards.

We _____ smoke.   We _____ sometimes work with a partner.

We _____ listen to tapes.   We _____ read our German books.

We _____ sleep!   We _____ .

6

 2:22

Tom is on the phone to his mother and father. They want to go and see Tom at the campsite tomorrow. Which is Tom's tent?

Can you remember what the things A–H are?
If you can't remember all of them, listen again.

Must, mustn't, have to

What must I / he / they do?		
I You He She We You They	**must**	come at 6 o'clock. go now. work on Saturdays.

What mustn't you / she / we do?		
I You He She We You They	**mustn't**	smoke here. drive over 30. do that!

I You	**don't have to**	work today, it's Sunday. finish it today, there's always tomorrow. walk, there's a bus.
He She	**doesn't have to**	
We You They	**don't have to**	

Do I Do you Does he	have to go there now?

Yes,	I do. you do. he does.

No,	I don't. you don't. he doesn't.

Unit seventeen – the seventeenth unit

1a

 2:23

21

A lady is at the ticket office of her local station. She'd like to buy a ticket from London to Aberdeen.

Good morning, can I help you?

Yes, I'd like to go to Aberdeen.

When would you like to go?

On Friday. Which station does the train leave from?

From King's Cross, platform 8.

Thank you. Oh, how much is the fare?

Single or return?

Return, please.

Do you want first class or second?

Second class, please.

That's £104, second class return.

Okay, here you are.

Thank you, and here's your ticket. Have a good journey.

Thank you, goodbye.

1b

The lady with red hair wants to go to Aberdeen on Friday. What must she do?

e.g. She must buy a ticket.

go reserve buy go find out pack pay	a newspaper to read. her things. a seat. to the station. £104 to the platform. the time of the train.

This is her seat: 8   What mustn't she do here?

2a

🔘 2:24

There are some people at the ticket office. Listen to what they say and write in the information here. The information about Aberdeen is from the dialogue in 1a.

	Aberdeen		Brighton		Dover		Cambridge		Bristol		York		Bath	
Victoria														
Charing Cross														
King's Cross	✓													
Paddington														
Liverpool Street														
single / return	S	Ⓡ	S	R	S	R	S	R	S	R	S	R	S	R
class	1st	2nd	1st	2nd	1st	2nd	1st	2nd	1st	2nd	1st	2nd	1st	2nd
fare £	104													
passenger														

Info 2009:
Standard train tickets are more expensive now, but you can also find more special offers.

2b

Put these words in the correct order to make questions about the passengers and the journeys:

a) Which   leave   does   train   Aberdeen   station   to   the   from?

_____

b) How   journey   the   long   to   is   Aberdeen?

_____

c) Would   like   first   second   the   a   or   passenger   class   ticket?

_____

d) Does   want   single   a   or   passenger   the   return   a   ticket?

_____

e) How   the   is   much   fare?

_____

2c

Ask your partner the questions from 2b about Brighton, Dover, Cambridge, Bristol, York and Bath.

2d   Complete this fare table. You can find some of the information in 2a and your teacher has got the rest of the information. Ask:

How much is the *first/second class single/return* fare to York / Bath ... ?

London to:				Aberdeen	Brighton	Dover	Cambridge	Bristol	York	Bath
£	1st	→		78					40	21.70
		⇄						49.80		
£	2nd	→				9.50	7.30			
		⇄			13.80					

3a   These people are sitting in a train, in a second class compartment. They're going to Aberdeen. It's a long way from London to Aberdeen. What are they doing to pass the time? The woman in seat number eight is looking out of the window. The man opposite her, in seat number one, is sleeping. What are the other people doing?

The man	in seat number __ is	talking listening looking writing knitting eating reading sleeping.	a letter. a sandwich. a pullover. out of the window. a newspaper. to a friend. to music.
The woman			

3b   Is he ... ?   Is she ... ?

e.g. Is the man in seat number three listening to music?   Yes, he is.
Is the woman in seat number six reading a book?   No, she isn't.

4

Freedom of SCOTLAND ROVERS

WHERE YOU WANT · WHEN YOU WANT

How much is a Silver Ticket for an adult?

How much is a Silver Ticket for a child of 10?

How long is a Silver Ticket valid?

How much is a Gold Ticket for a child of 3?

How long is a Gold Ticket valid?

How much is a Gold Ticket for an adult?

Is it possible to go to a station in England with a Freedom of Scotland Rover ticket?

Can dogs travel free?

Silver Ticket	
VALID 7 DAYS	£38.00
Second Class	
Gold Ticket	
VALID 14 DAYS	£55.00
Second Class	

This covers:
1. All stations in Scotland and over the border to Carlisle and Berwick-upon-Tweed.
2. The Firth of Clyde sailings of Caledonian MacBrayne Ltd.
Freedom of Scotland Rovers for children aged 5 and under 16 are charged at half the adult price, children under 5 travel free. Dogs and prams go at half price.

Info 2009:
These tickets are now called "Freedom of Scotland Pass".
You can travel on 4 days in 8 for £111 oder for 8 days in 15 for £148.

Present continuous: he, she

He**'s going** to Scotland.	**Is** he **going** to Aberdeen?	Yes, he **is.**
He**'s reading** a book.	**Is** he **reading** a French book?	No, he **isn't.**

She**'s listening** to music.	**Is** she **listening** to pop music?	No, she **isn't.**
She**'s writing** a letter.	**Is** she **writing** to her sister?	Yes, she **is.**

Unit eighteen – the eighteenth unit

1a The radio amateur: Code GKA379

Bert is very interested in radios. He has got a huge radio at home and he can speak and listen to people from all over the world. He always listens with headphones, and he sometimes listens in the middle of the night. It's 5 o'clock in the morning now, and he's talking to a friend in Australia – it's 3 o'clock in the afternoon there!

1b

Listen to Bert's conversation with Ted in Australia and mark the correct words in this text.

2:25

Ted's code is
☐ BKE270.
☒ VKE270. He lives in
☐ VKl270.

☐ Sydney.
☐ Melbourne. His wife is in
☐ Brisbane.

☐ Sydney
☐ Melbourne today,
☐ Brisbane

she's visiting her
☐ mother
☐ brother in hospital. Ted is sitting in his
☐ friend

☐ office,
☐ bedroom, and
☐ garden,

is drinking a
☐ cup of tea.
☐ bottle of beer. His three children are
☐ glass of wine.

☐ with their mother.
☐ at school.
☐ at home.

The two boys are playing
☐ tennis
☐ cards   in the garden, and Ted's daughter is reading
☐ football

a
☐ book
☐ newspaper in the house. The sun
☐ letter

☐ is shining
☐ isn't shining   at the moment, but everyone is

happy because it's
☐ hot,
☐ warm, and it
☐ cold,

☐ is raining.
☐ isn't raining.

1c

Fill in the missing words here and write the correct answers:

e.g. _Is_ Bert speaking to Ted in Australia?   _Yes, he is_ .
Are Ted's children _speaking_ to Bert?   _No, they aren't_ .

a) _____ Ted's wife visiting her brother?   _____ .

b) _____ Ted _____ a cup of tea?   _____ .

c) _____ the children visiting their grandmother?   _____ .

d) _____ the boys _____ cards?   _____ .

e) _____ Ted's daughter reading a book?   _____ .

f) _____ she _____ a newspaper?   _____ .

g) _____ the sun _____ in Melbourne?   _____ .

h) _____ it raining?   _____ .

i) _____ Ted and Bert _____ on the phone?   _____ .

2a

What's he doing?   What's she doing?

e.g. What's your father doing now?   I think he's working in his office.
I think he's reading the newspaper at home.

Ask your partner about:

a) mother or father
b) brother or sister
c) grandmother or grandfather
d) Mr Pinzelli (page 14)

e) Alan (page 42)
f) Frank (page 55)
g) the Queen of England
h) the President of Switzerland

What does he think she's doing? What does she think he's doing?
But ...

2b

What are they doing?

The time now in our classroom is _____ o'clock.

Write about each place in this table.

e.g. In Moscow it's ... o'clock in the morning. The children are working at school.
In New York it's ... o'clock in the morning. The bankers aren't working in their banks, they're sleeping.

place	time difference	time	people	activity
London	− 1 hour			work
New York	− 6 hours		the bankers	learn
Honolulu	− 12 hours		the children	sleep
Moscow	+ 2 hours		the housewives	cook
Bombay	+ 5 hours		most people	eat
Sydney	+ 9 hours		the teachers	go
				. ? .

2c

 2:26
 22

Make a dialogue.

A: Hello ... is that Melbourne? This is London.

B: Hello ... yes, this is Ted in Melbourne.

A: Hello Ted. What's the weather like in Australia?

B: The sun's shining at the moment, and it's very warm.

A: And how are you, Ted?

B: Oh ... not too bad, thanks, and you?

A: I'm very well, thanks.

Paris / France	
Moscow / Russia	
Bombay / India	
New York / America	
Hamburg / Germany	
Rome / Italy	
Lucerne / Switzerland	

How are you?
Not too bad ...
Very well ...
Fine ...
Ok ...

3a   Bert can also talk to people in England on his radio. He usually knows when his friends are at home, or when they're working. But today everything is different. Today is a public holiday. Today is Monday, but most people aren't working.

usually

today

Bert usually wears a suit and tie on Mondays   – but today he's wearing a red pullover.
He usually works at the bank on Mondays   – but today he's playing golf.
His friends usually teach on Mondays   – but today they're playing golf with Bert.

Today is the best Monday this month for Bert and his friends!

3b   The girl in this picture is a hotel receptionist in a five star hotel.

She usually
– wears a uniform
– works at the hotel
– eats lunch alone
– eats lunch in the hotel
  restaurant
– reads a book at lunchtime
– drinks mineral water with
  her lunch.

How is today different?

4   The verbs with *ing* at the end come into one of these three groups:

1			2		3	
walk	walking		driv**e**	driving	swim	swi**mm**ing
speak	speaking					
play	playing		phon**e**	phoning	rob	ro**bb**ing
ski	skiing					

Sort these verbs from units 17 and 18 into their groups:

1	do *doing*		write _____		drink _____		learn _____
	talk _____		read _____		play _____		wear _____
	sit _____		sleep _____		shine _____		knit _____
	listen _____		go _____		rain _____		
	eat _____		visit _____		work _____		

5a   **What are the people doing?**

 2:27   *e.g. He's sleeping.*

a) They _____   e) She _____

b) He _____   f) They _____

c) She _____   g) He _____

d) He _____   h) She _____

5b   Write sentences about Bert and his wife:

e.g. Bert's wife plays tennis every Friday.
      Bert's wife is working in the garden now.

WHO	WHAT	WHEN
Bert's wife	play tennis	every Friday.
Bert's wife	work in the garden	now.
Bert	learn German	at the moment.
Bert	read his German book	right now.
Bert and his wife	eat in restaurants	three times a week.
Bert and his wife	eat at home	today.
Bert's wife	work in a boutique	every day.
Bert	cook the dinner	on Fridays.
Bert	talk to Australia	once a week.
Bert	not talk to Australia	now.

Present continuous: I, you, we, they

What	am I are you is he is she are we are you are they	doing?

I'm You're He's She's We're You're They're	phoning a friend. watching TV. learning English. swimming. writing a letter.

Am I speaking too fast?
Is he learning English?
Are you going to the pizzeria?

Yes, you are.
Yes, he is.
Yes, I am. / Yes, we are.

No, you aren't.
No, he isn't.
No, I'm not. / No, we aren't.

Unit nineteen – the nineteenth unit

1a   A letter from Claire

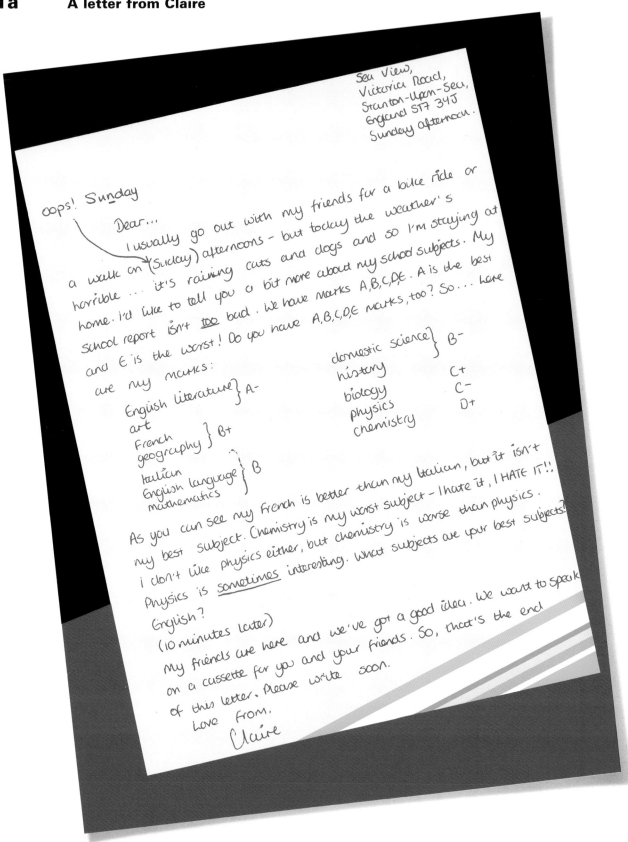

Sea View,
Victoria Road,
Stanton-Upon-Sea,
England ST7 34J
Sunday afternoon.

oops! Sunday

Dear ...
I usually go out with my friends for a bike ride or a walk on (Sunday) afternoons – but today the weather's horrible ... it's raining cats and dogs and so I'm staying at home. I'd like to tell you a bit more about my school subjects. My school report isn't too bad. We have marks A,B,C,D,E. A is the best and E is the worst! Do you have A,B,C,D,E marks, too? So ... here are my marks:

English literature } A-
art
French
geography } B+
Italian
English language } B
mathematics

domestic science } B-
history   C+
biology   C-
physics   D+
chemistry

As you can see my French is better than my Italian, but it isn't my best subject. Chemistry is my worst subject – I hate it, I HATE IT!! I don't like physics either, but chemistry is worse than physics. Physics is sometimes interesting. What subjects are your best subjects? English?

(10 minutes later)
My friends are here and we've got a good idea. We want to speak on a cassette for you and your friends. So, that's the end of this letter. Please write soon.
Love from,
Claire

1b Look at Claire's marks and complete these sentences:

a) _____ _____ *and* _____ are Claire's best subjects.

b) _____ is Claire's worst subject.

c) French is Claire's _____ foreign language.

d) _____ is Claire's best mark.

e) D+ is Claire's _____ _____ .

f) Claire's physics is better than her _____ .

g) Claire's French is worse than her *and* _____ _____ _____ .

h) Claire's history is _____ _____ her geography.

i) Claire's biology mark isn't good, but it's _____ _____ her physics mark.

j) Claire _____ chemistry.

2a Fill in the information that you hear on Claire's cassette.

2:28

	Claire	Paul	Elizabeth	Jim
How tall?	1.62 m			
How old?		14 y 2 m		
How heavy?			55 kg	
Best subject?	Eng. lit			
Worst subject?				art

Now compare the four friends:

taller than	/ the tallest	younger than	/ the youngest
shorter than	/ the shortest	heavier than	/ the heaviest
older than	/ the oldest	lighter than	/ the lightest

2b Work in groups of four. Ask questions and write the information here: your name: ↓

* How tall?				
* How old?				
* How heavy?				
Best subject?				
Worst subject?				

* Make a group report on these three questions. Compare the four people in the group.

3a

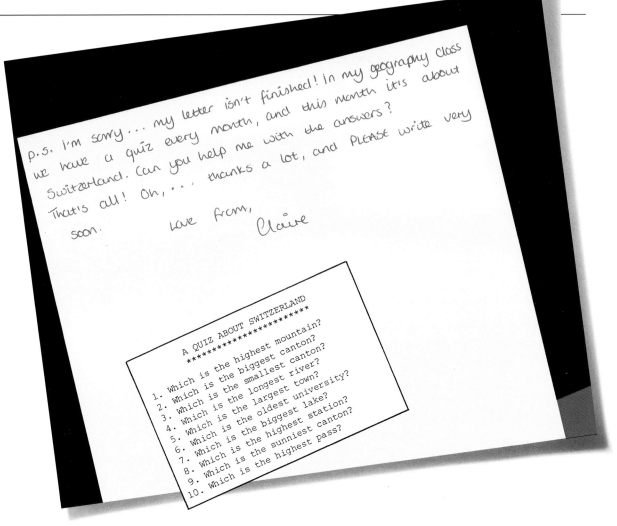

p.s. I'm sorry... my letter isn't finished! In my geography class we have a quiz every month, and this month it's about Switzerland. Can you help me with the answers? That's all! Oh,... thanks a lot, and PLEASE write very soon.

Love from,
Claire

A QUIZ ABOUT SWITZERLAND
****
1. Which is the highest mountain?
2. Which is the biggest canton?
3. Which is the smallest canton?
4. Which is the longest river?
5. Which is the largest town?
6. Which is the oldest university?
7. Which is the biggest lake?
8. Which is the highest station?
9. Which is the sunniest canton?
10. Which is the highest pass?

3b Write to Claire. Tell her about your subjects at school, and answer her questions about Switzerland.

4a

🔘 2:29

Listen to Claire, she's talking to one of her friends on the phone. She's got some information for one of their geography quizzes. Answer these five questions:

1. Which of these islands is the largest?
☐ Great Britain ☐ Madagascar ☐ Cuba

2. Which of these seas is the biggest?
☐ Black Sea ☐ Red Sea ☐ Mediterranean

3. Which of these continents is the largest?
☐ North America ☐ Africa ☐ South America

4. Which of these mountains is the highest?
☐ Mount Kenya ☐ Weisshorn ☐ Mont Blanc

5. Which of these rivers is the longest?
☐ Volga ☐ Yangtze Kiang ☐ Amazon

4b

2:29

Listen to Claire again, and write down the numbers she says.
The islands, the seas and the continents are in **square kilometres** (sq.km.).
The mountains are in **metres** (m.), and the rivers are in **kilometres** (km.).

1. _____ sq.km.   _____ sq.km.   _____ sq.km.

2. _____ sq.km.   _____ sq.km.   _____ sq.km.

3. _____ sq.km.   _____ sq.km.   _____ sq.km.

4. _____ m.   _____ m.   _____ m.

5. _____ km.   _____ km.   _____ km.

4c

Look at the information you've got about the islands, seas, continents, mountains and rivers
in exercise 4b. Compare them using *isn't as … as.*

e.g. Cuba – Great Britain   *Cuba isn't as large as Great Britain.*
Great Britain – Madagascar   *Great Britain isn't as large as Madagascar.*

a) the Black Sea – the Mediterranean
b) North America – Africa
c) the Weisshorn – Mount Kenya
d) the Volga – the Amazon

Write one sentence with *isn't as … as* about e) Claire f) Paul g) Elizabeth and h) Jim in
exercise 2a.

Comparatives and superlatives: short words

A is tall.	B is tall**er** than A.	C is the tall**est.**
A is young.	B is young**er** than A.	C is the young**est.**
A is nice.	B is nice**r** than A.	C is the nice**st.**
A is big.	B is big**ger** than A.	C is the big**gest.**
A is happy.	B is happ**ier** than A.	C is the happ**iest.**
A is heavy.	B is heav**ier** than A.	C is the heav**iest.**
A is a good student.	B is **better** than A.	C is the **best** student.
A is a bad singer.	B is **worse** than A.	C is the **worst** singer.

A isn't **as tall as** B.	B isn't **as tall as** C.
A isn't **as good as** B.	B isn't **as good as** C.

Unit twenty – the twentieth unit

1a Colin and Donna live in Nottingham – a town about 200 kilometres north of London. Colin's got a new job at Gatwick Airport, south of London. So, they're looking for a new flat – nearer to the airport. They don't want to buy a house because they both work and they haven't got time to look after a garden. Colin would like to live in London, but Donna wants to live in Brighton because it's by the sea. She'd like to find a job in a language school.

2:30

23

Colin: But Donna, the airport is nearer London than Brighton – and there's a train every 15 minutes from Victoria.

Donna: Yes, I know – but there are trains from Brighton to Gatwick, too. Let's go to Brighton next weekend and have a look. You don't know Brighton!

Colin: Well, I know I'd like to live in London. It's more interesting and more exciting than Brighton ... you can do everything there.

Donna: Yes, you can – but it's also a very expensive city, a lot more expensive than Brighton. We aren't millionaires! Brighton's smaller and quieter than London and ...

Colin: ... not in the summer when all the tourists come!

Donna: Oh, it's always quieter than London – the tourists go to London too, all year round. I think the most important question for us is money – and Brighton *is* cheaper than London, a lot cheaper.

Colin: Okay, let's go to Brighton next weekend and ...

Donna: ... oh good ... you know, I'm sure Brighton is the place for us.

1b What do you know about Colin and Donna's problem?

	TRUE	FALSE	DON'T KNOW
a) They live in Nottingham.	X		
b) They don't like Nottingham.			
c) Nottingham is nearer Gatwick Airport than London.			
d) They are looking for a house to buy.			
e) They don't want a garden.			
f) Colin wouldn't like to live in London.			
g) Colin thinks London's more exciting than Brighton.			
h) Donna would like to live by the sea.			
i) Donna's got a job in a language school in Nottingham.			
j) Colin's got a car.			
k) Colin knows Brighton.			
l) There are trains to Gatwick from London and from Brighton.			
m) The most important question for Donna is the distance from the airport.			

2a
 2:31

Colin and Donna are at an estate agent's called The Brighton Property Office. The man who works there is asking them some questions. Fill in his form:

THE BRIGHTON PROPERTY OFFICE

34 Sea Road
Brighton • Tel. 57 90 46

Open Mondays–Fridays 9 a.m. – 8 p.m.
Saturdays 10 a.m. – 5.30 p.m.
Sundays 2 p.m. – 4 p.m.

NAME: *C & D Blake*   (THIS FORM IS FOR FLATS ONLY)

Number of rooms   ... bedrooms   ... other rooms
- ☐ separate kitchen
- ☐ bathroom + toilet
- ☐ central heating
- ☐ garage
- ☐ basement flat

- ☐ gas kitchen
- ☐ separate bathroom and toilet
- ☐ gas fires
- ☐ garden
- ☐ ground floor flat

- ☐ electric kitchen
- ☐ electric fires
- ☐ higher than ground floor

Price
- ☐ up to £30,000
- ☐ £40,000–£50,000
- ☐ £60,000 +

- ☐ £30,000–£40,000
- ☐ £50,000–£60,000

Info 2009:
House prices in Brighton are much higher now, but you can buy a garage for under £30,000!

2b

Write a short description of the flat that Colin and Donna would like to have. Here are some words you can use:

They would like ...
They would like to have ...
They want ...
They want to have ...
They're looking for ...

They wouldn't like ...
They wouldn't like to have ...
They don't want ...
They don't want to have ...
Their flat must have ...

3a

Here are four descriptions of flats in Brighton:

The Brighton Property Office
- ground floor flat
- 3 bedrooms
- 1 living room
- 1 dining room
- central heating
- year: 1963
- 5 mins from sea
- 5 mins from shopping centre

- £ 188,000

The Brighton Property Office
- first floor flat
- 2 large bedrooms
- 1 large living room
- electric fires
- near shopping centre
- 10 mins from sea
- year: 1955

- £ 143,650

The Brighton Property Office
- basement flat
- 2 bedrooms
- 1 living room
- 1 dining room
- central heating
- sep. toilet
- year: 1932
- garage

- £ 148,400

The Brighton Property Office
- second floor flat
- 2 bedrooms
- 1 living room
- bathroom + toilet
- gas fires
- 15 mins from sea
- 10 mins from shopping centre
- year: 1895

- £ 139,800

Which of these flats has got the most bedrooms? *The* _____

Which of these flats is under £ 140,000? _____

Which of these flats is more than eighty years old? _____

Compare the flats using these words:

a) bigger than
b) smaller than
c) the biggest
d) the smallest

e) more expensive than
f) the most expensive
g) more modern than
h) the most modern

i) cheaper than
j) the cheapest
k) older than
l) the oldest

Which of these flats do you think is the best flat for Colin and Donna?

3b

 2:32

Colin and Donna are looking at the ground floor flat, the most expensive one. They know it's too expensive for them but they want to see it.

What are the rooms A–I?

A _____

B _____

C _____

D _____

E _____

F _____

G _____

H _____

I _____

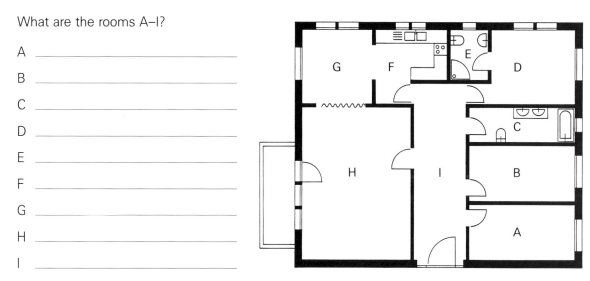

4

Find exercise 4a on pages 49 and 50 of this book. Ask questions about the things you can see there.

e.g. Is the English dress cheaper than the Italian dress?   Yes, it is.
Is the French car more expensive than the American car?   No, it isn't.

Write the questions about the dresses, the cars, the men and the hotels on a piece of paper – and give the paper to your partner who can write the answers to your questions.

Comparatives and superlatives

Longer words

A is interesting.	B is **more interesting** than A.	C is **the most interesting.**
A is expensive.	B is **more expensive** than A.	C is **the most expensive.**
A is modern.	B is **more modern** than A.	C is **the most modern.**

Short words

A is old.	B is **older** than A.	C is **the oldest.**
A is cheap.	B is **cheaper** than A.	C is **the cheapest.**

Unit twenty-one – the twenty-first unit

Revision unit

1a   What can you see here?
Write the words next to the things:

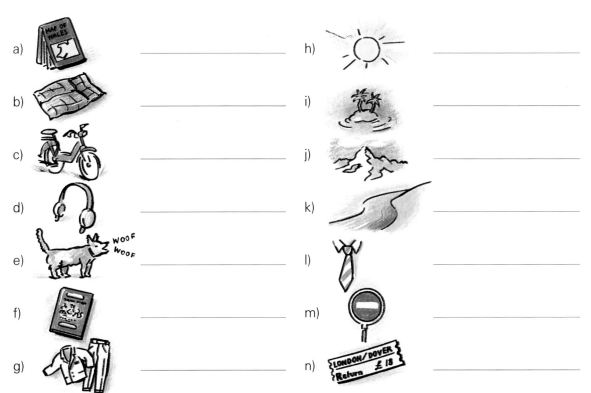

a) _____   h) _____

b) _____   i) _____

c) _____   j) _____

d) _____   k) _____

e) _____   l) _____

f) _____   m) _____

g) _____   n) _____

1b   What are these school subjects?

che_____   dom_____

bio_____   Ita_____

phy_____   mat_____

Eng_____   geo_____

Eng_____   his_____

Fre_____   a_____

2   Write these sentences again and replace the underlined words with *him, her, us* or *them:*

e.g. Do you know George?   Do you know him?

a) I must see Maria and Tony tomorrow.

b) Would you like to have dinner with George and me on Sunday?

c) Mr Pinzelli can see Mr Smith at eleven o'clock.

d) Please give Mary this book.

e) Do you think we can help Anna?

f) They always go to the swimming pool with the children on Saturdays.

g) They want to interview Mr Jones and his brother.

h) I'd like to have lunch with Peter on Friday.

i) Ask Mrs Davison.

j) Please phone my sister and me at about ten o'clock, okay?

3

Find the sentences:

We must

We mustn't

We don't have to

a) go by train, we've got a car.
b) go to school on Saturday mornings.
c) find eight sentences here.
d) drive on the right in Switzerland.
e) read our English books every day.
f) drive on the right in England.
g) speak English on Sundays.
h) smoke in the cinema.

| MUST + a ⓑ c d e f g h | MUSTN'T + a b c d e f g h | DON'T HAVE TO + a b c d e f g h |

4a

What are the people doing in these pictures?

e.g. 1. They're listening to the radio.

    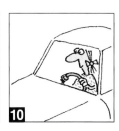

Here are the verbs for this exercise:

I S K _ski_

V D I R E _____

C W T A H _____

N S L E T I _____

K R W O _____

N K T I _____

E E S L P _____

L N A R E _____

Y L A P _____

W M S I _____

4b

Write sentences about these people:

e.g. Susan usually drinks tea, but she's drinking coffee at the moment.

	USUALLY	TODAY / NOW / AT THE MOMENT
Susan	drink tea	drink coffee.
1. Fred	walk to the office	go by bus.
2. John and Mary	eat at home	eat in a restaurant.
3. Sally	watch television	listen to a concert.
4. John	write to Sally	phone her.
5. Mr and Mrs Smith	stay at home	visit their daughter.

Now write two questions about these people. The answers must always be *No, …*

e.g. Does Susan usually drink coffee?   No, she doesn't.
Is Susan drinking tea today?   No, she isn't.

4c

Which verb is correct?

George Baker is a film star, but he isn't working at the moment. He is on holiday at Buntines in Tunis, for two weeks. At the moment he IS SITTING / SITS by the swimming pool with his wife, Janet. She usually WORKS / IS WORKING in a newspaper office – but she DOESN'T WORK / ISN'T WORKING now, she DRINKS / IS DRINKING a glass of very good wine … mm! It's good that they ARE HAVING / HAVE a holiday this week because next week they MUSTN'T / MUST both work.

5a

What are the first words of these questions? (They're all different!)

1. _____ is your birthday?

2. _____ old are you?

3. _____ money have you got here?

4. _____ is your favourite singer?

5. _____ brothers and sisters have you got?

6. _____ colour do you like best – red or green?

7. _____ is your mother / father / brother / sister at the moment?

8. _____ is your mother / father / brother / sister doing now?

9. _____ are you here in the classroom now?

10. _____ you like these questions?

5b   Now ask these questions to your partner.

6a

Write short sentences for these pictures:

e.g. Joe's car is small.   *Lyn's car is smaller.*   *Tim's car is the smallest.*

TIM JOE FRED

tall

interesting

SUE CAROL DIANA

expensive

heavy

big

6b

The Guinness Book of Records

3:1   Match the numbers and the words:

the smallest woman: _____   the largest garage: _____

the tallest man: _____   the highest station: _____

the oldest man: _____   the biggest hotel: _____

the heaviest man: _____   the longest train: _____

the highest number of children
(1 mother): _____

What are these numbers exactly? Metres? Kilos? … ?

538
6
114
59   69
2.72
9,250   4,786
3,200

7

Write these words in the correct sentences:

at (4 x)   for (2 x)   from (2 x)   in (2 x)   on (2 x)   to (3 x)

a) He comes _____ Jacksville.

b) Listen _____ what he's saying.

c) He's going _____ Paris today.

d) They're looking _____ a new flat.

e) Open your book _____ page 3.

f) Don't come _____ Friday.

g) Look _____ John – he's sleeping!

h) He works _____ his father.

i) They're camping _____ Scotland.

j) Breakfast is _____ 8 o'clock.

k) Ssh – He's _____ the phone.

l) The train leaves _____ platform 3.

m) He's interested _____ radios.

n) He often talks _____ a friend in Australia.

o) The children are _____ home.

Unit twenty-two – the twenty-second unit

1a

3:8
24

Kim: 375 4691, hello.

Sue: Hi Kim … listen would you like to come to my party?

Kim: Your party? It isn't your birthday, is it?

Sue: No … it isn't – I'd like to give a small party, that's all.

Kim: When is it?

Sue: A week on Saturday, that's the 17th.

Kim: The 17th? Oh Sue, I'm sorry, I can't come – I'm going to visit my grandparents in Bristol that weekend, I must go – it's their 50th wedding anniversary.

Sue: Oh, what a pity … I mean it's a pity you can't come to the party.

Kim: And what on earth can I give them? I just don't know. Mum and dad are going to buy them a colour television, and my brother's going to invite them to London. They're going to stay for a weekend and see a musical. But I don't know what I can buy them. Have you got a good idea for a present for them?

Sue: Mm … no. I don't know. Why don't we meet for a coffee this afternoon? We can talk about it then.

Kim: Fine, which coffee bar shall we meet in – Oasis or Casablanca?

Sue: Oasis, I think … at 3 o'clock?

Kim: I'd prefer 3.30.

Sue: Okay, see you there at 3.30.

Kim: Bye, see you later.

1b **Complete these questions and answer them.** These are the verbs for the last boxes in the questions: buy, see, give, stay, meet, visit

1. When ☐*is* Sue ☐*going to* ☐*give* a party?

On _*Saturday the 17th.*_ .

2. Who ☐ Kim ☐*going to* ☐ in Bristol?

Her _____ .

3. What ☐ Kim ☐ ☐ her grandparents?

She _____ .

4. What ☐ Kim's parents ☐ ☐ for them?

A _____ .

5. How long ☐ they ☐ ☐ in London?

For a _____ .

6. What ☐ they ☐ ☐ in London?

A _____ .

7. Where ☐ Kim and Sue ☐ ☐ for a coffee?

In _____ .

8. What time ☐ they ☐ ☐ this afternoon?

At _____ .

1c **Make a dialogue.**

3:9

25

A: Would you like to come to my party?

B: Oh yes … when?

A: On Saturday.

B: Oh, I'm sorry … I'm going to visit my grandparents on Saturday.

A: Oh, what a pity!

– play tennis with me
– come to the cinema with me
– have lunch with me
– come to the disco with me
– come for a bike ride with me
– have a pizza with me
	– on Monday
	  on Tuesday
	  on …
	– next weekend
	– on Friday evening
	– tomorrow
		– babysit for my cousin
		– have dinner with the Jones
		  family
		– play table tennis
		– help my father
		– watch videos with 3 or 4
		  friends
		– visit my sister in hospital

2a It's going to be an expensive month for Jill and Simon. They must buy a lot of presents. They're going to buy a wedding anniversary present for Jill's parents, a birthday present for her brother, a wedding present for Simon's sister, birthday presents for their twins (Mark and Kate), a thank you present for their neighbour (Mrs Lee) and a goodbye present for Simon's secretary.

🔊 3:10 Listen to Simon and Jill. Which of these presents are for which people? Write in the date and the number of the present for each person on this list.

	date	present
Jill's parents		
Jill's brother		
Simon's sister		

	date	present
their twins		
Mrs Lee		
Simon's secretary		

2b   Write about the presents.

e.g. Jill's parents / a watch *They aren't going to buy them a watch.*
Jill's brother / a book *They're going to buy him a book.*

a) Simon's sister / wine glasses
b) Mark / a camera
c) Kate / a watch
d) Mrs Lee / a plant
e) Simon's secretary, Sharon / a bottle of perfume
f) Jill's brother / a cassette
g) Sharon / a box of chocolates
h) Mrs Lee / a bottle of wine

3a   A letter from Claire

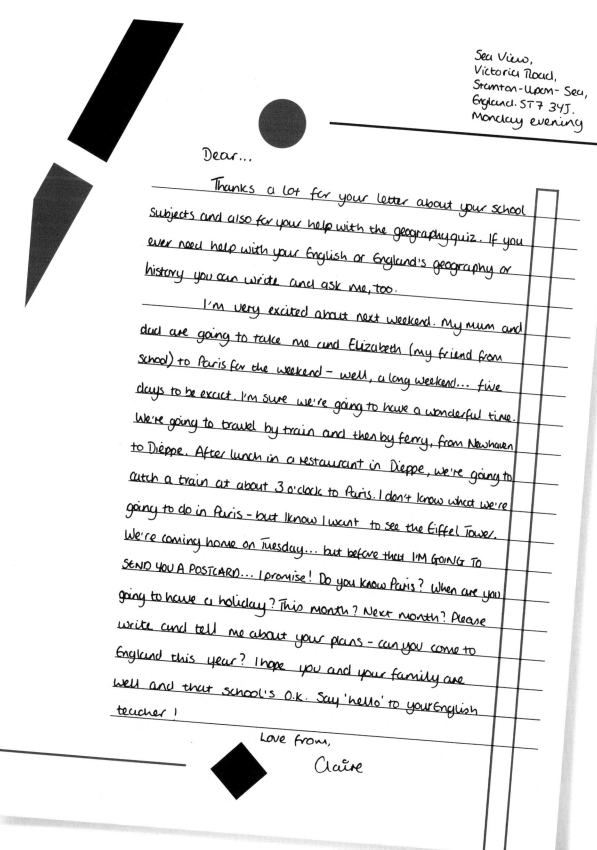

Sea View,
Victoria Road,
Stanton-Upon-Sea,
England. ST7 3YJ.
Monday evening

Dear...

Thanks a lot for your letter about your school subjects and also for your help with the geography quiz. If you ever need help with your English or England's geography or history you can write and ask me, too.

I'm very excited about next weekend. My mum and dad are going to take me and Elizabeth (my friend from school) to Paris for the weekend – well, a long weekend... five days to be exact. I'm sure we're going to have a wonderful time. We're going to travel by train and then by ferry, from Newhaven to Dieppe. After lunch in a restaurant in Dieppe, we're going to catch a train at about 3 o'clock to Paris. I don't know what we're going to do in Paris – but I know I want to see the Eiffel Tower. We're coming home on Tuesday... but before that I'M GOING TO SEND YOU A POSTCARD... I promise! Do you know Paris? When are you going to have a holiday? This month? Next month? Please write and tell me about your plans – can you come to England this year? I hope you and your family are well and that school's O.K. Say 'hello' to your English teacher!

Love from,
Claire

3b

The verb *to go* is special. Look:

She's going (to go) to Paris next week. = She's going to Paris next week.
They're going (to go) to London tomorrow. = They're going to London tomorrow.

Write these sentences:

e.g. She / Paris next week / see her friend
She's going to Paris next week, and she's going to see her friend there.

a) They / London tomorrow / watch a film.
b) We / the park next Saturday / play football.
c) I / the boutique on Friday / buy a pullover.
d) She / the English lesson tomorrow morning / ...
e) They / the football stadium this evening / ...
f) He / the Italian restaurant at 8 o'clock / ...

3c

Write to Claire and tell her about your plans for your next weekend or your next holiday.

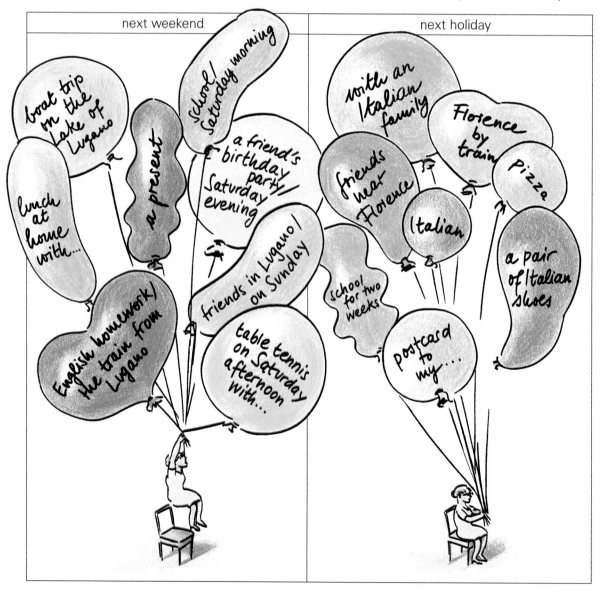

4

Ask your partner these questions with *going to:*

What
Where
What time
When

ARE YOU GOING TO

do next weekend?
do your homework?
finish school tomorrow?
have a holiday?
do after the English lesson?
eat this evening?
drink tomorrow morning?
wash your hair?
get up tomorrow?

Ask your teacher these questions too.

The future: going to

I'm You're He's She's We're You're They're	going to	do the work buy one see the house read the book eat it visit him talk to her	tomorrow. next week. later. next weekend.

Are you going to Paris tomorrow?
Is he going to travel by train?
Are they going to see him tomorrow?

Yes, I am.
Yes, he is.
Yes, they are.

No, I'm not.
No, he isn't.
No, they aren't.

I'm not going to Paris tomorrow.
He isn't going to travel by train.
They aren't going to see him tomorrow.

Unit twenty-three – the twenty-third unit

1a   *Thinking Back* is a radio programme. People who are older than seventy speak on the programme about when they were young. First you can hear Muriel Golding speaking about her twenties when she was a nurse.

3:11
26

When I was young I was a nurse in a large hospital. The work was hard, and the days were very long. My friends at the hospital, doctors and nurses, were from many different countries. My best friend was a girl called Lisa – she was from Ireland. She was two or three years younger than I was, and we were friends for years. I don't know where she is now – perhaps she's back in Ireland. Yes, life was hard then, but we were happy.

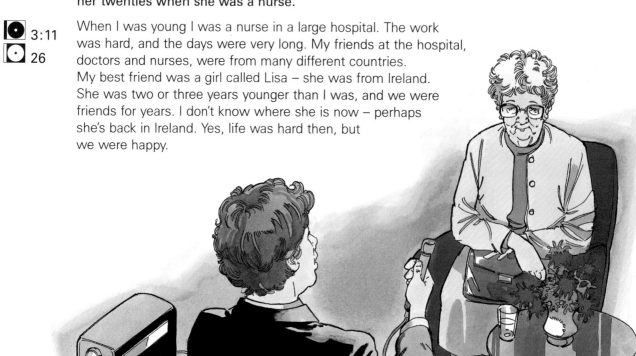

1b   The interviewer on the radio is asking Muriel about her family and her house. Write the words *was* or *were* in the gaps:

3:12

INT: What can you remember about your old house? Is it still there?

MURIEL: I don't know if it's still there – but I can remember the house – it _____ a small

house, but the garden _____ long with a lot of trees in it. We _____ five children in our

family, three boys and two girls. My brothers _____ all better at school than me.

INT: _____ you good friends with your sister?

MURIEL: Yes, we _____ the youngest in the family. I _____ the fourth of five children.

My father _____ a bus driver, and we _____ poor. It _____ sometimes very difficult

for my mother with five children, I can tell you. But my mum and dad _____ always happy.

I think it _____ nice that we _____ a big family.

1c   Answer these questions about Muriel:

e.g. *Was she a nurse when she was young?*   Yes, she was. / *No, she wasn't.*
Were all her friends from Ireland?   Yes, they were. / No, they weren't.
Was the hospital small?   Yes, it was. / No, it wasn't.

a) Was Muriel a doctor?   _____ .

b) Was the work in the hospital hard?   _____ .

c) Were the days short for Muriel?   _____ .

d) Were all her friends English?   _____ .

e) Was her best friend from Scotland?   _____ .

f) Was her friend called Lisa?   _____ .

g) Were they happy at the hospital?   _____ .

Now write in the first word of the question and the answer.

h) _____ Muriel's house small?   _____ .

i) _____ all Muriel's brothers older than her?   _____ .

j) _____ Muriel the youngest child?   _____ .

k) _____ Muriel's father a train driver?   _____ .

l) _____ they poor?   _____ .

m) _____ life easy for Muriel's mother?   _____ .

n) _____ Muriel's parents unhappy?   _____ .

2a   **Muriel's birthday party**

3:13   When was Muriel's birthday?   _____ .

How old was she?   _____ .

Where was her party?   At _____ .

Who was at the party? Write a number:

brother(s) _____   sister(s) _____   daughter(s) _____   son(s) _____

friend(s) _____   granddaughter(s) _____   grandson(s) _____

How many women and girls were there at the party? _____

How many men and boys were there at the party?   _____

2b

What was there on the table at Muriel's birthday party?

As you can see, there was a bottle of orange juice but there wasn't a bottle of mineral water. There were some wine glasses but there weren't any beer glasses.

Ask questions about the things in the list below:

e.g. bottle of apple juice   *Was there **a** bottle of apple juice?*
                               No, there wasn't.
       wine glasses   *Were there **any** wine glasses?*
                               Yes, there were.

sandwiches	birthday cake	chocolate cake	beer glasses
pot of tea	pot of coffee	apples	bottle of mineral water
eggs	small plates	cups and saucers	bottles of beer
small cakes	large plates	bottle of orange juice	bananas and oranges

2c

bottle of orange juice   *There was **a** bottle of orange juice.*
bottle of mineral water   *There wasn't **a** bottle of mineral water.*
wine glasses   *There were **some** wine glasses.*
beer glasses   *There weren't **any** beer glasses.*

Write sentences for these words:

a) apples
b) pot of coffee
c) eggs

d) sandwiches
e) small cakes
f) chocolate cake

g) bottles of beer
h) birthday card
i) letters

3a   Ask your partner questions beginning with *Where were you ... ?* Make a note of the answers.

e.g. *on your birthday*
Where were you on your birthday?
I was in London.

in London

a) yesterday evening at 7

b) this morning at 3 o'clock

c) on the 31st of December at midnight

d) last Sunday afternoon

e) yesterday afternoon at 2 o'clock

3b   Now write some sentences about your partner:

e.g. *... was in London on his/her birthday*

4a   **Where was he/she last Saturday?**   **What was ... like?**
          Where were they last Saturday?   **What were ... like?**

e.g. A: *Where was Carol last Saturday?*   A: *What was the film like?*
     B: *She was at the cinema.*   B: *It was very boring.*

at a party
the people: very interesting

Belinda

at the cinema
the film: very boring

Carol

at the opera
the singers: bad

Mr and Mrs Davison

at a concert
the music: fantastic

Sandra and Karin

in London
the weather: not too bad

George's sister

in Tunis
the hotel: very modern

Fred and Tanya

at a football match
the players: very good

George

at a restaurant
the food: excellent

Mr Pinzelli

on a train
the other people: very friendly

Bert and Tina

at the hairdresser's
her hair: awful

Mona

4b   Write sentences about the people in exercise 4a.

e.g. *Carol was at the cinema last Saturday, and the film was very boring.*

Was / were

I	was			I	wasn't	
You	were			You	weren't	
He/she/it	was	in our classroom yesterday.		He/she/it	wasn't	here last Sunday.
We You They	were			We You They	weren't	

Were you at home?	Yes, I was.
Was he at school?	No, he wasn't.
Were they good?	Yes, they were.
Were they here?	No, they weren't.

Was like / were like

What was the hotel like?	It was very nice. It wasn't too old.
What were the people like?	They were very interesting.
What were the singers like?	They weren't very good.

Some / any

+	−
There was **a** man in the shop.	There wasn't **a** woman.
There were **some** boys in the park.	There weren't **any** girls.

?

Was there **a** man in the shop?	Yes, there was.
Was there **a** woman in the shop, too?	No, there wasn't.
Were there **any** boys in the park?	Yes, there were.
Were there **any** girls in the park, too?	No, there weren't.

Which birthday card would you like to send?

Unit twenty-four – the twenty-fourth unit

1a *Quiz Time* is a general knowledge quiz programme that is on television once a week. Four students from Southend Comprehensive School and four from Bristol are in the final.

3:14

27

- Welcome to the last part of today's quiz. Now, Southend Comprehensive please think before you answer. Bristol have got three correct answers, and I've got five questions for you ... four must be correct to win. Ok? Four must be correct. Question one: When did the American astronaut Neil Armstrong first walk on the moon?
- Erm ... in 1969.
- Right. Well done. Number two: In which country did Picasso live when he was a child?
- In Spain.
- Right again! And here comes question three: When did the Second World War end?
- I think it was in – er – 1945 – yes it was – 1945.
- That's correct. You've got three answers right. You only need one more to win. So, question four: What did Alexander Bell invent in 1876?
- The electric light.
- Oh, no, I'm sorry ... no, he didn't invent the electric light ... no, he invented the telephone. Oh, bad luck. Well, there's still one more question. You must get this one right! Last question: In which American state did the first space shuttle land?
- I know, it was California.
- Right, well done! You've got four questions correct and so the team from Southend Comprehensive School are the winners. And the prize? Well, the space shuttle landed in California, and that's where you can go – for two weeks – to sunny California!

1b   Ask these questions. Use *did* or *didn't* in the answers.

e.g. *Did the students from Southend Comprehensive
      School win the quiz?*   *Yes, they did.*
      Did they get all the answers right?   *No, they didn't.*

Did the students from Bristol get four answers right?   _____ .

Did Neil Armstrong _____ on the moon in 1969?   _____ .

_____ Picasso live in Italy when he was a child?   _____ .

_____ Picasso _____ in Spain when he was a child?   _____ .

_____ the Second World War _____ in 1939?   _____ .

_____ Alexander Bell _____ the electric light?   _____ .

_____ Alexander Bell _____ the telephone?   _____ .

_____ the space shuttle _____ in California?   _____ .

1c   Ask your partner five questions (or more) about yesterday.

e.g. *Did you watch TV yesterday?*   *No, I didn't.*

      Did you drink a cup of coffee yesterday?   *Yes, I did.*

Here are some verbs: eat, drink, read, write, go, see, play, buy …

2a   Think about the quiz that was on television. Which words are missing at the beginning of these questions?

a) _____ did Armstrong first walk on the moon?   In 1969.

b) _____ did Picasso live when he was young?   In Spain.

c) _____ did the Second World War end?   In 1945.

d) _____ did Alexander Bell invent?   The telephone.

e) _____ did the space shuttle land?   In California.

f) _____ the students from Southend win the quiz?   Yes, they did.

2b   Ask questions beginning with the these words. Give very short answers only.

e.g. *Where did you buy your pullover?*   *In Italy.*

Here are the words to start your questions:
a) Where …   b) When …   c) What …   d) What time …   e) Did …

Think of two questions (beginning with *Did* …) to ask your teacher about yesterday or last weekend.

3

Write these words in the correct order to make questions:

a)   time   bed   night?   What   go   did   to   you   last

b)   you   school   five?   you   when   Did   go   were   to

c)   on   quiz   Did   you   the   TV?   watch

d)   did   Where   live   you   you   were   child?   a   when

e)   have   you   dinner   Did   eat   home   restaurant?   at   a
     yesterday   or   you   did   in   evening

Ask your teacher these questions.

4a

Listen to the tape and write the dates next to the pictures.

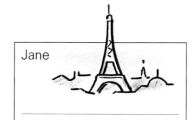

4b

Write one question for each picture in exercise 4a. The answers to all your questions must begin with *No, ...*

e.g. Did Jane go to Paris in 1938?   *No, she didn't.*

5a

The old lady in this photograph was born in England in the 19th century. Write ten sentences about things she didn't do then or things she didn't have then.

e.g. She didn't use a mobile phone.
She didn't have a plastic shopping bag.

5b

This is a conversation between the two people in the photo in 5a. Write the dialogue in your book. When you see * put a word in.

Here are the words you need: was (4x), were (3x), wasn't, weren't, did (5x), didn't (2x).

Girl: When * you born, grandma?
Old lady: Oh … I * born in 1865.
Girl: And where * you born?
Old lady: In Manchester.
Girl: * you go to school in Manchester?
Old lady: No, I *. I * only in Manchester for four years.
Girl: And then? * you go to London when you * four?
Old lady: No … no, we * go to London. We * very rich and London * too expensive for us.
Girl: So, where * you go?
Old lady: To Liverpool … Liverpool * too expensive … it * cheaper than London.
Girl: * you go to school in Liverpool?
Old lady: Yes, I *.

Past simple: questions with did, negative sentences

Did	I you he she we you they	go	to Scotland? to the cinema? alone?

Yes,	I you he/she we you they	**did.**

No,	I you he/she we you they	**didn't.**

I You He She We You They	**didn't** go	to Scotland. to the cinema. alone.

Unit twenty-five – the twenty-fifth unit

1a   A famous painter

3:16

28

Picasso was born in Malaga, Spain in 1881. His first name was Pablo. He lived in Malaga for ten years and then his family moved to Vigo in 1891 – they travelled there by boat. You can see these words on their house in Vigo: "Pablo Ruiz Picasso lived and painted in this house 1891–1895".

So he started very young, didn't he? His father was his teacher, and one day his father suddenly stopped painting and never painted again – his son was better. Pablo was the best artist in the Picasso family. Later, Picasso lived in France. He worked very hard and produced hundreds of paintings. He painted this painting of the Soler family in 1903, but his paintings changed a lot when he was older. Pablo Ruiz Picasso died in France in 1973.

1b   Write these words in the correct order to make questions:

a) Where   born   Picasso   was   ? _____*Where*_____ ?

b) What   Picasso   name   was   's   first   ?

   _*What*_____ ?

c) How long   Picasso   in   live   did   Malaga   ?

   _____ ?

d) When   family   the   did   move   Vigo   Picasso   to   ?

   _____ ?

e) How   travel   did   Vigo   they   to   ?

   _____ ?

f) Why   father   painting   did   stop   his   ?

   _____ ?

g) How many   Picasso   did   produce   paintings   ?

   _____ ?

h) Which   he   in   family   paint   did   1903   ?

   _____ ?

i) When   Picasso   die   did   ? _____ ?

1c   Now write the answers to these questions.

1d   Here are some questions beginning with *Who* ... Write in the missing words:

Who lived in Malaga for ten years?

Who moved to Vigo in _____ ?

_____ travelled by boat?

Who _____ in the house in Vigo?   PICASSO DID.

Who _____ in France?

_____ _____ hundreds of paintings?

_____ _____ in 1973?

Look back at 1a in Unit 24. Write 3 questions beginning with *Who* ...

_____ ? Armstrong did.

_____ ? Picasso did.

_____ ? Alexander Bell did.

2a The story of Picasso's life (1881–1973) is famous ... but the story of Jim Blogg's life (1900–1962) isn't famous. Jim Blogg was a lonely man.

LIVE	*He lived in London.*
WORK	
START	
FINISH	
WATCH TV (sometimes)	
LISTEN TO MUSIC (sometimes)	
VISIT FRIENDS (never)	
PLAY (never)	

2b Yes, Jim Blogg was a lonely man. He worked hard but he didn't have any friends.
That Friday the 13th, in 1962, was a bad day for Jim Blogg. What was different for him?

 travel by bus / walk to work   e.g. *He didn't walk to work, he travelled by bus.*

 start at 9.45 / start at 9

 have lunch / stay in his office

 read the newspaper / work hard all day

 finish at 7.15 / go home at 5

 eat in a snack bar / cook at home

 cook a fish / have a steak

But the fish was old,
The dinner was cold,
And poor Jim Blogg _____ (†) at midnight.

The moral of this story is:
Don't cook old fish on Friday the 13th.

2c Write questions about Jim Blogg and that Friday.

a) 3 questions which give positive answers
e.g. Did Jim travel to work by bus?   *(Yes, he did.)*

b) 3 questions which give negative answers
e.g. Did Jim walk to work?   *(No, he didn't.)*

c) 3 questions with the verbs *start, finish* and *cook* – and the word *or*
e.g. (verb: travel)   Did Jim travel by car or by bus?   (He travelled by bus.)

Now mix the order of the questions and ask them to your partner.

3a Can you hear a verb in the present or the past in these sentences?

3:17   PRESENT: *1*

PAST:

3b Listen to the sentences again. Are the verbs positive or negative?

3:17   POSITIVE:

NEGATIVE: *1*

3c Here are the sentences. What did you hear on the tape?

☐ *didn't live*
e.g. 1. Sentence was present/negative … He ☐ *lives*   *in London.*
☒ *doesn't live*

☐ play
2. They ☐ played   tennis yesterday
☐ didn't play   afternoon.

☐ didn't read   the newspaper in the
7. She ☐ reads   mornings.
☐ doesn't read

☐ didn't talk
3. We ☐ talked   to John at the party.
☐ don't talk

☐ speak
8. They ☐ don't speak   English there.
☐ didn't speak

☐ don't like
4. The children ☐ like   fish and chips.
☐ liked

☐ phoned
9. I ☐ don't phone   him yesterday.
☐ didn't phone

☐ worked
5. Jim Blogg ☐ works   in a small office.
☐ didn't work

☐ parks
10. He ☐ parked   his car there.
☐ doesn't park

☐ arrive
6. I ☐ didn't arrive   at the party before John.
☐ arrived

4   Make sentences with these verbs:

I, you, he, she, it, we, you, they	answered asked arrived cooked danced finished interviewed invented kidnapped knitted	landed listened lived looked parked played phoned rained robbed smiled	smoked started stayed talked travelled visited walked watched worked	**?**	yesterday. last week. on Monday. when he/she was young.

e.g. She answered Claire's letter last week.
 I asked three questions about her book yesterday.

5a   **Six famous men**

🔘 3:18   Listen to the information about these six men and write the name of their birthplaces and the dates when they were born and when they died in the boxes.

1. Pablo Picasso	*Malaga*	*1881*	*1973*
2. Charlie Chaplin			
3. Napoleon Bonaparte			
4. Wolfgang Amadeus Mozart			
5. John F. Kennedy			
6. John Lennon			

birthplaces:
Liverpool Salzburg
        Boston
Corsica London

they were born in:
1756 1769   1917
        1940 1889

they died in:
1963 1821 1791
    1980 1977

5b   There are three sentences about each man here. Match the sentences to the men. Picasso's first sentence has already got his number (1) next to it.

	He acted in films.		He was a painter.
	Someone murdered him when he was 46.		He was a politician.
	He lived in the 18th and 19th centuries.		He was an actor.
	He composed a lot of operas and concertos.		He was a pop singer.
	He didn't live to be 40 years old.		He died 10 years before Picasso.
1	He lived the longest of these 6 men.		He lived for 88 years.
	He died in the year of his fortieth birthday.		He painted hundreds of pictures.
	He was a composer of classical music.		Someone murdered him when he was 40.
	He died 30 years after Mozart.		He was a general in the army.

5c   Look at this question and the example answers:

What do you know about Picasso?   He was born in Malaga, *wasn't he?*
He was born in 1881, *wasn't he?*
He was a famous painter, *wasn't he?*

He lived in Spain, *didn't he?*
He painted a picture of the Soler family, *didn't he?*
He died in 1973, *didn't he?*

Now ask and answer the same question about Charlie Chaplin, Bonaparte, Mozart, John F. Kennedy and John Lennon.

5d   Ask questions beginning with *Who* ... Give a name only as the answer.

e.g. *Who was born in Malaga?*   *Picasso.*
Who was born in 1940?   *John Lennon.*
Who died in 1963?   *John F. Kennedy.*

Past simple: regular

What did he invent?	He **invented** the electric light.	He didn't invent the telephone.
What did he paint?	He **painted** pictures.	He didn't paint houses.
What did he kidnap?	He **kidnapped** the poodle.	He didn't kidnap the rich lady.
What did she knit?	She **knitted** a pullover.	She didn't knit a dress.
Where did she live?	She **lived** in Manchester.	She didn't live in London.
Where did they dance?	They **danced** at the disco.	They didn't dance in the park.

Unit twenty-six – the twenty-sixth unit

1a A winter holiday

Last February Claire's class went to St. Moritz for a winter holiday. She went skiing for the first time in her life. She was in the beginners' class, and she wasn't very good at skiing. She enjoyed her holiday very much, and liked St. Moritz, too. There was a lot of snow and St. Moritz looked wonderful with a beautiful blue sky every day. She'd like to go there again next year, but she must save some money first. Skiing holidays aren't cheap!

1b

When she was back at school in England, Claire and her friends worked on a project about their winter holiday... they made a cassette. They recorded an interview. Listen to their interview and choose the correct words in these sentences:

3:19   e.g. Claire went to St. Moritz with *her parents.*
                                              (*her class.*)

a) They came to Switzerland   by plane.
                              by train.

b) They stayed at a   small hotel.
                      youth hostel.

c) They stayed in St. Moritz for   ten days.
                                   a week.

d) Claire   bought   a pair of skis in St. Moritz.
            hired

e) They had skiing lessons every   morning.
                                   afternoon.

f) Claire fell over because she tried to   ski and talk at the same time.
                                           ski too fast.

g) They saw Prince Michael / the Cresta Run one day.

h) They ate fondue on the last evening. / twice.

i) Claire and her friends drank wine with the fondue. / every day.

j) Claire wrote postcards to all her friends. / her family.

k) Claire said "Au revoir" / "Auf Wiedersehen" to her ski instructor on the last day!

1c Read all of 1a+b again, and find the past of these verbs:

buy _____	have _____	enjoy _____
come _____	make _____	hire _____
drink _____	say _____	like _____
eat _____	see _____	stay _____
fall _____	write _____	try _____
go _____		work _____

1d

Write questions about Claire's holiday in St. Moritz. It must be possible to answer all your questions with *No, …*

e.g. Did Claire go to St. Moritz with her parents?　　*No, she didn't.*

Ask your questions to your partner. This time give longer answers.

e.g. Did Claire go to St. Moritz with her parents?
　　No, she didn't. She went with her class.

2a   These are some of the things Claire had in St. Moritz. Number the list below:

She took:

____ a long scarf

____ a bottle of suntan cream

____ a woollen hat

____ a pair of sunglasses

____ 7 pairs of warm socks

____ a ski overall

____ a German phrase book

____ her address book

____ a pair of boots

____ a pair of gloves

She hired:

____ a pair of goggles

____ a pair of skis

____ a pair of sticks

____ a pair of ski boots

2b

What did they forget?

Claire's friends all forgot to take some of these things to St. Moritz. Write two sentences about each person – the first sentence with *and* in the middle, and the second sentence with *but* in the middle.

	1	2	3	4	5	6	7	8	9	10
Jim	✗	✔	✗	✔	✔	✔	✔	✗	✔	✔
Elizabeth	✔	✔	✔	✔	✗	✔	✗	✔	✔	✔
Paul	✔	✗	✔	✗	✔	✔	✔	✔	✔	✗
Linda	✔	✗	✔	✔	✗	✔	✔	✔	✔	✗

e.g. Jim took a bottle of suntan cream with him, and he took a ski overall, too.
    Jim took his address book with him, but he didn't take his sunglasses – he forgot them.

Now write about Elizabeth, Paul and Linda.

3a   Combine these words to make questions:

When	see there
Where	travel
How	buy there
Where	stay
How long	take/hire/forget
What	go
What	stay there
What	have a holiday

1. *When did you have a holiday* ?
2. _____ ?
3. _____ ?
4. _____ ?
5. _____ ?
6. _____ ?
7. _____ ?
8. _____ ?

3b   Ask these questions to your partner.

3c   Here's a short report about Claire's sister. She had a holiday, too – but she didn't go skiing in St. Moritz.

Jane had a holiday last summer. She went to Penzance, that's in Cornwall in the southwest of England. She travelled by train. She stayed at a small hotel near the sea for two weeks. She bought a lot of postcards and a painting of the sea. Jane saw a lot of old houses in Cornwall, and she saw the 'First and Last House in England' in a place called Land's End. She enjoyed her holiday very much.

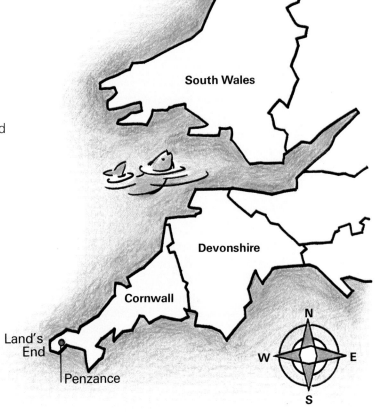

Now write a short report like this about your partner. Use the information from 3b.

4

 3:20

Listen to the sentences and questions on the tape. Are they in the past or in the present? Are they positive or negative sentences, or are they questions?

	1	2	3	4	5	6	7	8	9	10	11	12
past												
present	✓											
positive sentence	✓											
negative sentence												
question												

5

Talk about yesterday.

eat   write   drink   see   play   buy   phone   watch

e.g. A: I ate a pizza yesterday, and you Sonja?
B: I didn't eat a pizza, I ate a hamburger. And you Peter?
C: I didn't eat a pizza or a hamburger, I ate two eggs.

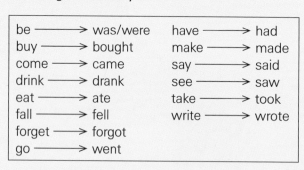

Past simple: irregular

Where **did** you **go?**	We **went** to Paris.	We **didn't go** to Zurich.
What **did** he **eat?**	He **ate** a pizza.	He **didn't eat** a hamburger.
What **did** they **drink?**	They **drank** coffee.	They **didn't drink** wine.

The irregular verbs you know:

be ⟶ was/were	have ⟶ had	Look at these verbs that end with 'y':
buy ⟶ bought	make ⟶ made	
come ⟶ came	say ⟶ said	
drink ⟶ drank	see ⟶ saw	enjoy ⟶ enjoyed
eat ⟶ ate	take ⟶ took	play ⟶ played
fall ⟶ fell	write ⟶ wrote	
forget ⟶ forgot		cry ⟶ cried
go ⟶ went		try ⟶ tried

NB. The past form is the same for all persons – it never changes
(exception: the verb 'be', see Unit 23).

Views of Cornwall and St. Moritz:

1. The coastline, Cornwall
2. A typical Engadine building, St. Moritz
3. The lake, St. Moritz
4. Fishing boats in St. Ives, Cornwall
5. Surfers on the lake, St. Moritz
6. The First and Last House in England, Cornwall

Unit twenty-seven – the last but one unit

1a The Story of Humphrey Hawkins

One Saturday Humphrey decided to go to a large department store in the centre of town. In what order do you think he did these things?

He

	parked his car.
	left the car park via the George Street exit.
	found a multi-storey car park.
1	drove to town.
	locked the car door.
	bought a newspaper in the newsagent's next to the car park.
	took a ticket at the entrance.
	got out of the car.
	went to the department store on foot.

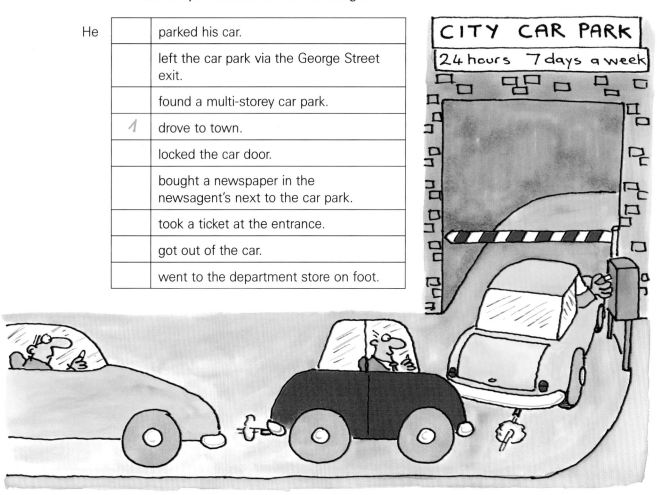

1b Match the questions and answers and write the missing verbs in the answers.

1. Did Humphrey walk to town?

2. Did he find a parking space in the street?

3. Did Humphrey take a ticket when he left the car park?

4. Did he get out of his car in the street?

5. Did Humphrey lock his car door?

6. Did he leave the car park via the entrance?

7. Did Humphrey buy a book in the newsagent's?

8. Did Humphrey go from the car park to the department store by bus?

___ a) No, he didn't, he _____ on foot.

___ b) Yes, he _____ .

___ c) No, he didn't, he _____ a newspaper.

_1_ d) No, he didn't, he _____ to town.

___ e) No, he didn't, he _____ one at the entrance.

___ f) No, he didn't, he _____ one in a multi-storey car park.

___ g) No, he didn't, he _____ _____ in the car park.

___ h) No, he didn't, he _____ via the George Street exit.

2a

3:21

Listen to the next part of "The Story of Humphrey Hawkins".
On this street plan you can see part of the centre of Humphrey's town.
What did Humphrey do at the places numbered 1–9?

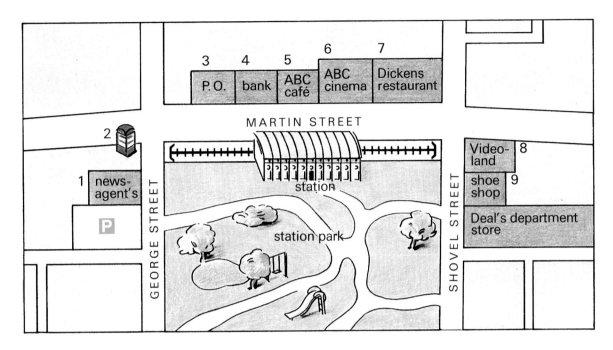

These are the verbs you need:
REGULAR: order, phone, post, reserve, try on
IRREGULAR: buy, drink, eat, find out, take out

1. _____ .
2. _____ .
3. _____ .
4. _____ .
5. _____ .
6. _____ .
7. _____ .
8. _____ .
9. _____ .

2b

Write 9 questions (about the 9 places on the plan) that give the answer *No, he didn't.*

e.g. 1. Did he buy a Swiss newspaper in the newsagent's.   *No, he didn't.*

3a

Put the words in these sentences in the correct order to continue "The Story of Humphrey Hawkins". All of the sentences begin with *she, he* or *Humphrey*.

to   Humphrey   floor   second   the   went

department   he   to   the   household   went

buy   wanted   machine   a   he   to   coffee

ten   saw   machines   he   different   coffee

the   coffee   he   know   which   best   didn't   machine   was

lady   he   shop   in   worked   who   asked   a   the

said   that   the   was   Coffee-2000   she   best   the

bought   the   he   Coffee-2000   home   went   and

a   he   cup   made   good   coffee   very   of   it   drank   and

3b

Then Humphrey decided to look at the instructions. He saw something very important.

make sure you always use filter coffee
of the best quality.

V E R Y   I M P O R T A N T
****

We want you to be happy and satisfied
with your brand new coffee machine
COFFEE-2000

For perfect results every time, use
your coffee machine every day – then
we can guarantee you an aromatic,
fresh-tasting cup of coffee.

Please fill in the card that is
box – giving your full
so that we can

3c

Now listen to the dramatic end of "The Story of Humphrey Hawkins".

 3:22

4a Before you finish Unit 27 and go on to the last revision unit … there are nine more irregular verbs that are very important to learn. Match the verbs on the left with the past forms in the circle.

bring _____   read _____

do _____   speak _____

give _____   tell _____

know _____   think _____

meet _____

met
gave
told spoke
knew read
           brought
thought did

4b Listen to these sentences about Humphrey, and write in the missing words:

 3:23

1. He _____ his mother about the coffee machine, but he _____ his father.

2. He _____ the guarantee, but he _____ the instructions.

3. He _____ the name of the shop, but he _____ the name of the woman who worked there.

4. He _____ all the work in the office, but he _____ all his housework.

5. He _____ his father on Sunday, but he _____ his mother.

6. He _____ to his brother about it, but he _____ the woman in the shop.

7. He _____ the coffee machine was very good, but he _____ the instructions were very clear.

8. He _____ his mother a birthday card, but he _____ her a present.

9. He _____ the machine to my house, but he _____ the instructions.

Past simple: irregular
There's a list of all the past forms that you know on page 170.

Now go on to Unit 28 – the last unit in this book!

Unit twenty-eight – the twenty-eighth unit

1　Complete these sentences
with the past of the verb in brackets ( ),
and two more words:

e.g. She _wanted_ a _bottle_ of _perfume_ . (want)

1. She _____ a _____ of _____ . (make)

2. He _____ a _____ of _____ . (drink)

3. They _____ her a _____ of _____ . (give)

4. She _____ a _____ of _____ . (hire)

5. We _____ a _____ of _____ . (eat)

6. He _____ a _____ of _____ . (find)

7. He _____ a _____ of _____ . (buy)

8. They _____ a _____ of _____ . (have)

9. She _____ a _____ of _____ . (see)

10. She _____ a _____ of _____ . (take)

11. He _____ a _____ of _____ . (try on)

12. They _____ to buy a _____ of _____ . (forget)

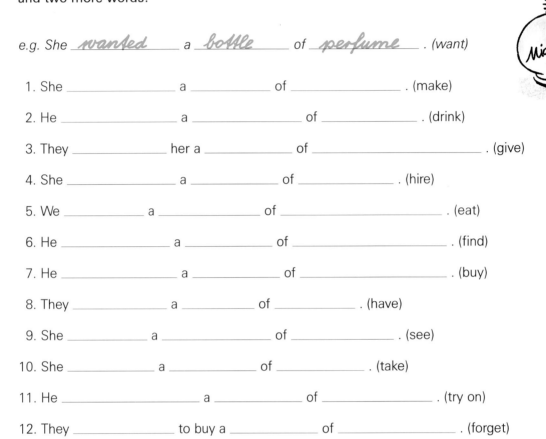

2a   These are Bert's plans for next week.

These are your plans – you and Bert are friends.

MY WEEK:
Tues. 19.30 table tennis
Wed. 2-5 tennis
Fri. MY BIRTHDAY!
Sat. (all day) visit Uncle Tom. 9.30 train → Nottingham

	MORNING	AFTERNOON	EVENING
M			
Tu			cinema with Bill + Jane 7p.m.
W		2-5 tennis with Bert	
Th			
F	(Bill + Jane → Geneva for the International Weekend)		Bert's birthday dinner – Dickens restaurant
Sa		lunch with Sandra (my house)	
Su	do my homework	visit Sue in hospital	Disco Futura

Answer these questions using *going to* in every answer:

a) What are you going to do on Tuesday evening?

  I'm going to the _____

b) Why can't Bert go to the cinema with you, Bill and Jane?

  Because _____

c) Can you and Bert visit Sue in hospital on Wednesday afternoon?

  _____ *because* _____

d) What time are you going to play tennis?

  _____

e) Can Bill and Jane have dinner with Bert on his birthday?

  _____ *because* _____

f) Can Bert visit Sandra at home on Saturday at about 12.30?

  _____ *because Sandra* _____

g) Is Bert going to have lunch with you on Saturday, too?

  _____ *because* _____

h) Have you got any plans for Sunday?

  _____

2b

It's now a week later. What did you do last week? Remember, you're Bert's friend.

e.g. Tuesday / go / cinema / Bill and Jane
   see / American film
   very good
   start / 7 o'clock
   finish / 9.30

On Tuesday evening, I went to the cinema with Bill and Jane. We saw an American film. It was very good. The film started at seven o'clock, and finished at half past nine.

1. Wednesday / tennis / Bert
   Bert / better / me
   play / three hours

2. Friday / Bill and Jane / go / Geneva / International Weekend
   Friday evening / dinner / Bert / restaurant / because …
   eat
   drink
   buy / for his birthday

3. Saturday / Sandra / come / lunch / my house
   stay / 3 hours
   watch video after lunch

4. Sunday / do homework
   Sunday / visit Sue / hospital
   a lot better
   Sunday / the disco / go / bed / midnight

3

Complete this short poem with the words *was* or *were*.

It _____ midnight by the river

I _____ cold

They _____ old

He _____ tall

They _____ small

He _____ here and

We _____ near

The river

And it _____ midnight.

   (G.R. London)

4

 3:24

Colin and Donna went out for the day last Saturday. Listen to the tape and answer these questions by writing one word:

1. Where did they go for the day last Saturday?   To _____ .
2. How did they travel?   By _____ .
3. What did Colin read on the train?   A _____ .
4. What did Donna write on the train?   A _____ .
5. What time did the train get to Victoria?   At _____ .
6. What did Colin and Donna try to find outside the station? A _____ .
7. Where did the driver drive them to?   The _____ Museum.
8. What did Colin and Donna say in the museum?   _____ .
9. What did they see in the museum?   _____ rooms.
10. Where did they meet again 2 hours later?   In the _____ .
11. What did they eat in Covent Garden?   A _____ .
12. What did they drink there?   A glass of _____ .
13. What time did they leave Covent Garden?   At _____ .
14. Which train did they take from Victoria?   The _____ train.

Now write long answers so that you can tell the story of Colin and Donna's day in London. Begin with: *On Saturday, Colin and Donna went to London. They ...*

5   Fill in the missing words in this table of past forms:

arrive	– _____	find	– _____	_____	– phoned
be	– _____	_____	– forgot	play	– _____
bring	– _____	get	– _____	read	– _____
_____	– bought	_____	– gave	rob	– _____
come	– _____	go	– _____	_____	– said
_____	– danced	have	– _____	see	– _____
_____	– died	kidnap	– _____	speak	– _____
_____	– did	_____	– knew	_____	– took
drink	– _____	leave	– _____	tell	– _____
drive	– _____	live	– _____	think	– _____
_____	– ate	make	– _____	travel	– _____
enjoy	– _____	_____	– met	try	– _____
fall	– _____	paint	– _____	write	– _____

6   Write these words in the sentences:

by   for   from   of (3x)   at (4x)   on (5x)   in (5x)   to (5x)

a) Would you like to come _____ my party?

b) I'm going to visit my friends who live _____ Bristol.

c) I visited them _____ Saturday.

d) They're going to travel _____ train.

e) There were 20 people _____ the party.

f) They drank 10 bottles _____ orange juice.

g) He invented the electric light _____ 1876.

h) They watched the quiz _____ TV.

i) They went _____ bed at midnight.

j) He was born _____ Spain.

k) He walked _____ the office.

l) They arrived _____ the party _____ 7 o'clock.

m) She forgot to phone him _____ his birthday.

n) Claire wasn't very good _____ skiing.

o) She stayed in the youth hostel _____ ten days.

p) She hired a pair _____ skis.

q) Penzance is _____ the southwest _____ England.

r) He went _____ the car park _____ the shop _____ foot.

s) He tried _____ a pair of black shoes _____ the shoe shop.

t) She said 'goodbye' _____ her teacher.

7

Yesterday was a bit different for Tony. He didn't do all the things he usually does. Write about what he did yesterday.

*e.g. Tony usually gets up at 7 o'clock.
He got up at 5 o'clock yesterday.*

1. He usually eats breakfast in a snack bar near his office.
2. He usually drinks coffee in the mornings.
3. He usually reads the newspaper in the mornings.
4. He usually leaves home at 7.45.
5. He usually takes a small bag with him.
6. He usually meets a man from the office at the bus stop.
7. He usually travels by bus in the mornings.
8. He usually arrives at the office at 8.10.
9. He usually speaks to his secretary when he arrives.
10. He goes to the office every day.

8   What did Humphrey Hawkins do after he saw the tea-maker in Deal's? To find out what he did, write all the words in the puzzle (going down ↓). Then find the word across (→) in each block.

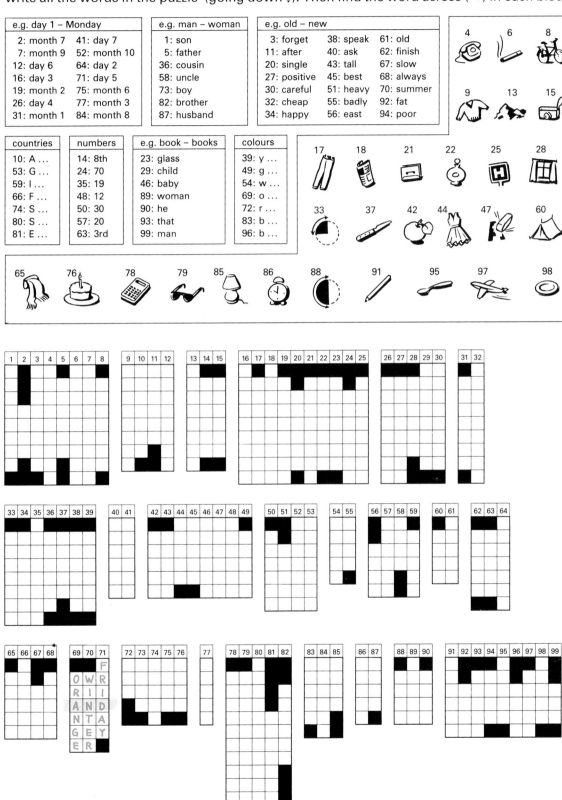

e.g. day 1 – Monday	
2: month 7	41: day 7
7: month 9	52: month 10
12: day 6	64: day 2
16: day 3	71: day 5
19: month 2	75: month 6
26: day 4	77: month 3
31: month 1	84: month 8

e.g. man – woman
1: son
5: father
36: cousin
58: uncle
73: boy
82: brother
87: husband

e.g. old – new		
3: forget	38: speak	61: old
11: after	40: ask	62: finish
20: single	43: tall	67: slow
27: positive	45: best	68: always
30: careful	51: heavy	70: summer
32: cheap	55: badly	92: fat
34: happy	56: east	94: poor

countries
10: A …
53: G …
59: I …
66: F …
74: S …
80: S …
81: E …

numbers
14: 8th
24: 70
35: 19
48: 12
50: 30
57: 20
63: 3rd

e.g. book – books
23: glass
29: child
46: baby
89: woman
90: he
93: that
99: man

colours
39: y …
49: g …
54: w …
69: o …
72: r …
83: b …
96: b …

Appendix

Unit-by-unit word list

Unit one

1
a centre for students (ə 'sentə fə 'stjuːdnts)	ein Zentrum für Schüler
It's in Wales. (ɪts ɪn 'weɪlz)	Es ist in Wales.
the first day (ðə 'fɜːst 'deɪ)	der erste Tag
international summer camp (ˌɪntə'næʃnl 'sʌmə kæmp)	internationales Sommerlager
She's from Wales. ('ʃiːz frəm 'weɪlz)	Sie ist von Wales.
She's the receptionist. ('ʃiːz ðə rɪ'sepʃənɪst)	Sie ist die Empfangsdame.
at the centre (ət ðə 'sentə)	im Zentrum
England ('ɪŋglənd)	England
Scotland ('skɒtlənd)	Schottland
Northern Ireland ('nɔːðn 'aɪələnd)	Nordirland
United Kingdom (juː'naɪtɪd 'kɪŋdəm)	Vereinigtes Königreich

2a
What's your name, please? ('wɒts jɔː 'neɪm pliːz)	Wie heissen Sie, bitte?
My name's … (maɪ 'neɪmz)	Ich heisse …
Where are you from? ('weə ə juː 'frɒm)	Woher kommen Sie?
I'm from … ('aɪm frəm)	Ich komme aus …

2b
He's a student, too. ('hiːz ə 'stjuːdnt 'tuː)	Er ist auch Schüler.
Italy ('ɪtəlɪ)	Italien
Italian (ɪ'tæljən)	Italiener(in), italienisch
Germany ('dʒɜːmənɪ)	Deutschland
German ('dʒɜːmən)	Deutsche(r), deutsch
France (frɑːns)	Frankreich
French (frentʃ)	Franzose / Französin, französisch
Spain (speɪn)	Spanien
Spanish ('spænɪʃ)	Spanier(in), spanisch
Switzerland ('swɪtsələnd)	Schweiz
Swiss (swɪs)	Schweizer(in), schweizerisch
Great Britain ('greɪt 'brɪtn)	Grossbritannien
British ('brɪtɪʃ)	britisch

3a
Where's she from? ('weəs ʃiː 'frɒm)	Woher kommt sie?

3b
colour(s) ('kʌlə[z])	Farbe(n)
flag(s) (flæg[z])	Fahne(n)
red (red)	rot
white (waɪt)	weiss
blue (bluː)	blau
black (blæk)	schwarz
green (griːn)	grün
yellow ('jeləu)	gelb

Unit two

1a
Hello everybody. (hələu 'evrɪˌbɒdɪ)	Guten Tag miteinander.
Welcome to … ('welkəm tə)	Willkommen in …
This is a plan … ('ðɪs ɪz ə 'plæn)	Dies ist ein Plan …
here (hɪə)	hier
Tent A is next to … ('tent 'eɪ ɪz 'neks tə)	Zelt A ist neben …
snack bar ('snæk bɑː)	Imbissecke
entrance ('entrans)	Eingang
toilet(s) ('tɔɪlɪt[s])	WC
washroom(s) ('wɒʃruːm[z]))	Waschraum
They're (are) here. ('ðe ə [ɑː] 'hɪə)	Sie sind hier.
boy(s) / girl(s) (bɔɪ[z] / gɜːl[z])	Knabe(n) / Mädchen

1b
What's this? ('wɒts 'ðɪs)	Was ist das?

1c   with (wɪð)   mit

2a   on unit one (ɒn 'ju:nɪt 'wʌn)   in der ersten Lektion
    book ('bʊk)   Buch

2c   Excuse me … (ɪks'kju:z mi:)   Entschuldigen Sie …
    I'm sorry. (aɪm 'sɒrɪ)   Es tut mir Leid.
    I don't know. (aɪ 'dəʊn 'nəʊ)   Ich weiss es nicht.
    Thank you. ('θæŋkjʊ)   Danke.

3a   evening ('i:vnɪŋ)   Abend
    photo ('fəʊtəʊ)   Foto
    friend (frend)   Freund
    garden (('gɑ:dn)   Garten
    hotel (həʊ'tel)   Hotel
    school (sku:l)   Schule
    car (kɑ:)   Auto
    teacher ('ti:tʃə)   Lehrer(in)
    class / classroom (klɑ:s / 'klɑ:srʊm)   Klasse / Klassenzimmer
    film (fɪlm)   Film

4a   breakfast ('brekfəst)   Frühstück
    lunch (lʌntʃ)   Mittagessen
    dinner ('dɪnə)   Nachtessen
    tray (treɪ)   Tablett
    fork (fɔ:k)   Gabel
    glass (glɑ:s)   Glas
    cup (kʌp)   Tasse
    menu ('menju:)   Speisekarte
    spoon (spu:n)   Löffel
    saucer ('sɔ:sə)   Untertasse
    plate (pleɪt)   Teller
    chair (tʃeə)   Stuhl
    knife (naɪf)   Messer
    table ('teɪbl)   Tisch
    apple ('æpl)   Apfel
    ashtray ('æʃtreɪ)   Aschenbecher
    egg (eg)   Ei
    orange ('ɒrɪndʒ)   Orange

Unit three

1a   new receptionist ('nju: rɪ'sepʃənɪst)   neue Dame / neuer Herr am Empfang
    The manager must find … (ðə 'mænɪdʒə məst 'faɪnd)   Der Direktor muss … finden
    Mr Pinzelli ('mɪstə pɪn'zelɪ)   Herr Pinzelli
    three people ('θrɪ 'pi:pl)   drei Leute
    interview ('ɪntəvju:)   Interview, Vorstellungsgespräch
    She can't speak French. (ʃi 'kɑ:nt 'spi:k 'frentʃ)   Sie kann nicht Französisch (sprechen).
    Can she type? ('kæn ʃɪ taɪp)   Kann sie Maschine schreiben?
    write shorthand ('raɪt 'ʃɔ:thænd)   stenografieren
    drive a car ('draɪv ə 'kɑ:)   Auto fahren
    start next month ('stɑ:t neks 'mʌnθ)   nächsten Monat beginnen

2a   ride a bicycle ('raɪd ə 'baɪsɪkl)   Velo fahren
    use a computer (ju:z ə kəm'pju:tə)   einen Computer benützen
    play football ('pleɪ 'fʊtbɔ:l)   Fussball spielen
    sing (sɪŋ)   singen
    ski (ski:)   Ski fahren
    make coffee ('meɪk 'kɒfɪ)   Kaffee machen
    swim (swɪm)   schwimmen
    cook spaghetti ('kʊk spə'getɪ)   Spaghetti kochen

Unit-by-unit word list

2b	group (gruːp)	Gruppe

3a	sister ('sɪstə)	Schwester
	but (bət)	aber
	goldfish ('gəʊldfɪʃ)	Goldfisch
	fly (flaɪ)	fliegen
	baby ('beɪbɪ)	Säugling / Kleinkind
	cry (kraɪ)	weinen

3c	very well ('verɪ 'wel)	sehr gut
	badly ('bædlɪ)	(sie singt) schlecht

4a	blind (blaɪnd)	blind
	hospital ('hɒspɪtl)	Spital
	walk in the park ('wɔːk ɪn ðə 'paːk)	im Park spazieren
	watch television ('wɒtʃ ˌtelɪvɪʒn)	fernsehen
	phone a friend ('fəʊn ə 'frend)	einem Freund telefonieren
	read the newspaper ('riːd ðə 'njuːsˌpeɪpə)	die Zeitung lesen
	smile at people ('smaɪl ət 'piːpl)	Leute anlächeln
	eat fish and chips ('iːt 'fɪʃ n 'tʃɪps)	Fisch und Pommes frites essen
	in a restaurant (ɪn ə 'restərɒnt)	in einem Restaurant
	dance (daːns)	tanzen

4b	Why? Because … (waɪ bɪ'kɒz)	Warum? Weil …

Unit four

1a	secretary ('sekrətrɪ)	Sekretär(in)
	brother ('brʌðə)	Bruder
	all (ɔːl)	alle
	How many … have you got? ('haʊ 'menɪ … 'həv ju 'gɒt)	Wie viele … hast du?
	a big family (ə 'bɪg 'fæməlɪ)	eine grosse Familie
	only ('əʊnlɪ)	einzig, nur
	none (nʌn)	keine
	that's all ('ðæts ɔːl)	das ist alles

1b	an only child (ən 'əʊnlɪ 'tʃaɪld)	ein Einzelkind

2a	family tree ('fæməlɪ 'triː)	Stammbaum
	mother / father ('mʌðə / 'faːðə)	Mutter / Vater
	wife / husband (waɪf / 'hʌzbənd)	Ehefrau / Ehemann
	aunt / uncle (aːnt / 'ʌŋkl)	Tante / Onkel
	daughter / son ('dɔːtə / sʌn)	Tochter / Sohn
	cousin ('kʌzn)	Cousin(e)

2b	He's called Paul. (hiːz 'kɔːld 'pɔːl)	Er heisst Paul.

3	room (ruːm)	Zimmer

4	(numbers 1–9, page 168)	(Zahlen 1–9, Seite 168)
	number ('nʌmbə)	Zahl, Nummer

5	watch (wɒtʃ)	Armbanduhr
	man / men (mæn / men)	Mann / Männer
	woman / women ('wʊmən / 'wɪmɪn)	Frau / Frauen
	child / children (tʃaɪld / 'tʃɪldrən)	Kind / Kinder
	baby / babies ('beɪbɪ / 'beɪbɪz)	Säugling / Säuglinge
	see (siː)	sehen

Unit five

1a	interviewer ('ɪntəvju:ə)	Befrager
	radio ('reɪdɪəu)	Radio
	pop singer ('pɒp sɪŋə)	Popsänger(in)
	Who … ? (hu:)	Wer … ?
	her favourite city (hɜ 'feɪvərɪt 'sɪtɪ)	ihre Lieblingsstadt
	his favourite drink (hɪz 'feɪvərɪt 'drɪŋk)	sein Lieblingsgetränk
	food (fu:d)	Essen, Nahrung
	film star ('fɪlm sta:)	Filmstar
	tea (ti:)	Tee
	wine (waɪn)	Wein
	beer (bɪə)	Bier
2	hair (heə)	Haar(e)
	pullover ('puləuvə)	Pullover
	shoe (ʃu:)	Schuh
	trousers ('trauzəz)	Hose
	long (lɒŋ)	lang
	short (ʃɔ:7)	kurz
4	Can you give me … please? ('kæn ju 'gɪv mi: … pli:z)	Können Sie mir bitte … geben?
	I think so. (aɪ 'θɪŋk səu)	Ich glaube (es).
	Here you are. ('hɪə ju 'a:)	Da ist es. / Da haben wir es.
	pen (pen)	Füllfeder
	ruler ('ru:lə)	Massstab
	calculator ('kælkjuleɪtə)	Taschenrechner
	pencil ('pensl)	Bleistift
	rubber ('rʌbə)	Gummi
	dictionary ('dɪkʃənrɪ)	Wörterbuch
5	office ('ɒfɪs)	Büro
6a	house (haus)	Haus

Unit six

1a	at the cinema (ət ðə 'sɪnəmə)	im Kino
	What time is the film, please? (wɒt 'taɪm ɪz ðə fɪlm pli:z)	Wann beginnt der Film, bitte?
	5 o'clock ('faɪv ə'klɒk)	fünf Uhr
	That's good. ('ðæts 'gud)	Das ist gut.
	ticket ('tɪkɪt)	Billett
1b	£7 per ticket ('sevn 'paundz pə 'tɪkɪt)	£7 pro Billett
	concert ('kɒnsət)	Konzert
	opera ('ɒpərə)	Oper
	play (pleɪ)	Schauspiel, Theaterstück
1c	today (tə'deɪ)	heute
2a	now (nau)	jetzt
	our ('auə)	unser(e)
2b	letter ('letə)	Brief
	Dear … , (dɪə)	Liebe(r) …
	different ('dɪfrənt)	anders
	their (ðeə)	ihr(e)
	kiss (kɪs)	Kuss
3	this is ('ðɪs ɪz)	dies ist
	that is ('ðæt ɪz)	jenes ist

Unit-by-unit word list

4a	(numbers 11–20, page 168)	(Zahlen 11–20, Seite 168)
5a	these are ('ðiːz ə) those are ('ðəʊz ə)	dies sind jenes sind
6a	little ('lɪtl)	wenig
	… years old ('jɜːz 'əʊld)	… Jahre alt
	penfriend ('penfrend)	Brieffreund(in)
	Europe ('jʊərəp)	Europa
	hobbies ('hɒbɪz)	Hobbys
	swimming ('swɪmɪŋ)	Schwimmen
	reading ('riːdɪŋ)	Lesen
	playing tennis ('pleɪɪŋ)	Tennis spielen
	listening to music ('lɪsnɪŋ tə 'mjuːzɪk)	Musik hören
	love from ('lʌv frəm)	liebe Grüsse

Unit eight

1a	live (lɪv)	wohnen
	work in a bank ('wɜːk ɪn ə 'bæŋk)	bei einer Bank arbeiten
	go by bus ('gəʊ baɪ 'bʌs)	den Bus nehmen
	start at 9 o'clock ('stɑːt ət 'naɪn ə'klɒk)	um 9 Uhr beginnen
	finish ('fɪnɪʃ)	aufhören
	like (laɪk)	lieben, gern haben
	job (dʒɒb)	Beruf
1b	Mrs Johnson ('mɪsɪz 'dʒɒnsn)	Frau Johnson
2a	smoke (sməʊk)	rauchen
	cigar (sɪ'gɑː)	Zigarre
	put sugar in … (pʊt 'ʃʊgə ɪn)	Zucker nehmen in …
3a	boyfriend ('bɔɪfrend)	Freund
4a	(days of the week, page 168)	(Wochentage, Seite 168)
	cook dinner ('kʌk 'dɪnə)	Nachtessen kochen
	He learns French. (hiː 'lɜːns 'frentʃ)	Er lernt Französisch.
4b	on Mondays (ɒn 'mʌndɪz)	montags

Unit nine

1a	Look! (lʊk)	Schau!
	How often … ? ('haʊ 'ɒfn)	Wie oft … ?
	every day ('evrɪ 'deɪ)	jeden Tag
	week (wiːk)	Woche
	in the mornings ('ɪn ðə 'mɔːnɪŋz)	morgens
	in the afternoons ('ɪn ðɪ ˌɑːftə'nuːnz)	nachmittags
	in the evenings ('ɪn ðɪ 'iːvnɪŋz)	abends
	all the time ('ɔːl ðə 'taɪm)	immer
	write (raɪt)	schreiben
	once a month ('wʌns ə 'mʌnθ)	einmal pro Monat
	twice a week ('twaɪs ə 'wiːk)	zweimal pro Woche
2a	get up ('get ʌp)	aufstehen
	station ('steɪʃn)	Bahnhof
	arrive (ə'raɪv)	ankommen

3a	half past six ('hɑːf pɑːst 'sɪks)	halb sieben
3b	a quarter past six (ə 'kwɔːtə pɑːst 'sɪks) a quarter to six (ə 'kwɔːtə tə 'sɪks) minute ('mɪnɪt)	(ein) Viertel nach sechs (ein) Viertel vor sechs Minute
3c	Can you tell me … ? ('kæn jʊ 'tel miː)	Können Sie mir sagen … ?
4a	three times a day ('θriː 'taɪmz ə 'deɪ)	dreimal am Tag
5	always ('ɔːlweɪz) usually ('juːʒʊəlɪ) often ('ɒfn) sometimes ('sʌmtaɪmz) never ('nevə)	immer normalerweise oft manchmal nie
6a	do homework (dʊ 'həʊmwɜːk)	Hausaufgaben machen

Unit ten

1	boutique (buːˈtiːk) expensive (ɪkˈspensɪv) How much is it? ('haʊ 'mʌtʃ ɪz ɪt) pound (paʊnd) a bit expensive (ə 'bɪt ɪkˈspensɪv) the blue one (ðə 'bluː wʌn) cheap (tʃiːp) That's better. ('ðæts 'betə) May I … ('meɪ aɪ) try on ('traɪ 'ɒn) of course (əv 'kɔːs)	Boutique teuer Wie viel kostet es? Pfund ein bisschen teuer der Blaue billig Das ist besser. Darf ich … probieren selbstverständlich
2a	(numbers 10–101, page 168)	(Zahlen 10–101, Seite 168)
3	(the alphabet, page 168)	(das Alphabet, Seite 168)
4a	dress (dres) American (əˈmerɪkən) old (əʊld) new (njuː) fast (fɑːst) slow (sləʊ) young (jʌŋ) tall (tɔːl) short (ʃɔːt) fat (fæt) thin (θɪn) rich (rɪtʃ) poor (pʊə) modern ('mɒdən) small (smɔːl) big (bɪg)	Kleid amerikanisch alt neu schnell langsam jung gross (gewachsen) klein (gewachsen) dick dünn reich arm modern klein gross
4c	the opposite of (ðɪ 'ɒpəzɪt əv)	das Gegenteil von
4d	or (ɔː)	oder
5a	skirt (skɜːt)	Jupe
6	drink (drɪŋk)	trinken

Unit-by-unit word list

Unit eleven

1

disco ('dɪskəʊ)		Disco
come (kʌm)		kommen
near here ('nɪə 'hɪə)		in der Nähe
then (ðen)		denn, dann
ask a question ('ɑːsk ə 'kwestʃən)		eine Frage stellen
Go ahead. ('gəʊ ə'hed)		Ja, bitte, machen Sie das nur.
so many questions ('səʊ 'menɪ 'kwestʃənz)		so viele Fragen

4a

disc jockey ('dɪsk 'dʒɒkɪ)	Diskjockey
musical instrument ('mjuːzɪkl 'ɪnstrʊmənt)	Musikinstrument

6

When … ? (wen)	Wann … ?

7a

lunchtime ('lʌntʃtaɪm)	Mittagszeit
Tell me about … ('tel mɪ ə'baʊt)	Erzähl mir von …
my best friend (mɪ 'best 'frend)	mein bester Freund / meine beste Freundin
street (striːt)	Strasse
I'm not very good at … (aɪm 'nɒt verɪ 'gʊd ət)	Ich bin nicht sehr stark in …
Please write soon. ('pliːs 'raɪt 'suːn)	Schreib bald, bitte.
horrible mess ('hɒrəbl 'mes)	fürchterliches Durcheinander

8

there (ðeə)	dorthin
have (hæv)	haben

Unit twelve

1a

alone (ə'ləʊn)	allein
sit (sɪt)	sitzen
Would you like … ? ('wʊd ju 'laɪk)	Hättest du gerne … ? / Hätten Sie gerne … ?
thanks (θæŋks)	danke
I'd like … ('aɪd 'laɪk)	Ich hätte gerne …
orange juice ('ɒrɪndʒ 'dʒuːs)	Orangensaft
fine (faɪn)	gut
waiter ('weɪtə)	Kellner

1b

hot chocolate ('hɒt 'tʃɒkələt)	heisse Schokolade
mineral water ('mɪnərəl 'wɔːtə)	Mineralwasser
a pot of tea (ə 'pɒt əv 'tiː)	eine Kanne Tee
milk (mɪlk)	Milch
bottle ('bɒtl)	Flasche

2

hamburger ('hæmbɜːgə)	Hamburger
sandwich ('sændwɪdʒ)	Sandwich
more (mɔː)	mehr
cigarette (ˌsɪgə'ret)	Zigarette
order ('ɔːdə)	Bestellung

3a

pizzeria (ˌpiːtsə'rɪə)	Pizzeria
order ('ɔːdə)	bestellen

3b

something ('sʌmθɪŋ)	etwas
just a salad ('dʒʌst ə 'sæləd)	nur einen Salat
certainly ('sɜːtnlɪ)	selbstverständlich
… anything to drink? ('enɪθɪŋ tə 'drɪŋk)	… etwas zu trinken?
bring (brɪŋ)	bringen

4a

birthday cake	('bɜːθdeɪ 'keɪk)	Geburtstagskuchen
cassette	(kə'set)	Kassette
think	(θɪŋk)	denken
a good idea	(ə 'gʊd aɪ'dɪə)	eine gute Idee
say	(seɪ)	sagen

4b

(the months of the year, page 168)	(die Monate, Seite 168)
(ordinal numbers, page 168)	(Ordnungszahlen, Seite 168)

Unit thirteen

1a

place	(pleɪs)	Ort
nice	(naɪs)	schön, nett, hübsch
swimming pool	('swɪmɪŋ 'puːl)	Schwimmbad
tennis court	('tenɪs 'kɔːt)	Tennisplatz
weather	('weðə)	Wetter
cold	(kəʊld)	kalt
at home	(et 'həʊm)	daheim / zu Hause
there is	(ðə 'ɪz)	es hat / es gibt
there are	(ðə 'ɑː)	es hat / es gibt
crowded	('kraʊdɪd)	überfüllt
too smoky	('tu: 'sməʊkɪ)	zu rauchig
too much	('tu: 'mʌtʃ)	zu viel
bar	(bɑː)	Bar
video club	('vɪdɪəʊ 'klʌb)	Video-Klub
mini golf	('mɪnɪ 'gɒlf)	Minigolf

1d

lift	(lɪft)	Lift

1e

postcard	('pəʊstkɑːd)	Ansichtskarte

2a

window	('wɪndəʊ)	Fenster
a view of the sea	(ə 'vju: əf ðə 'sɪ)	Meersicht
picture	('pɪktʃə)	Bild
alarm clock	(ə'lɑːm 'klɒk)	Wecker
balcony	('bælkənɪ)	Balkon
bed	(bed)	Bett
bedside table	('bedsaɪd 'teɪbl)	Nachttisch
carpet	('kɑːpɪt)	Teppich
cupboard	('kʌbəd)	Kasten / Schrank
curtain	('kɜːtn)	Vorhang
drawer	(drɔː)	Schublade
lamp	(læmp)	Lampe
mirror	('mɪrə)	Spiegel
plant	(plɑːnt)	Pflanze
telephone	('telɪfəʊn)	Telefon
waste paper basket	('weɪst 'peɪpə 'bɑːskɪt)	Papierkorb

2b

bedroom	('bedrʊm)	Schlafzimmer

3b

want	(wɒnt)	wollen
holiday	('hɒlədɪ)	Ferien
stay	(steɪ)	bleiben
a night	(ə 'naɪt)	eine Nacht
pilot	('paɪlət)	Pilot
basketball	('bɑːskɪtbɔːl)	Basketball

Unit-by-unit word list

4a

quick (kwɪk)	schnell
right (raɪt)	richtig
understand (ˌʌndəˈstænd)	verstehen
concentrate (ˈkɒnsəntreɪt)	sich konzentrieren
look at (ˈlʊk ət)	anschauen
attractive (əˈtræktɪv)	attraktiv
excellent (ˈeksələnt)	hervorragend
make a mistake (ˈmeɪk ə mɪˈsteɪk)	einen Fehler machen
impossible (ɪmˈpɒsəbl)	unmöglich
words (wɔːdz)	Text
she speaks clearly (ʃɪ ˈspiːks ˈklɪəlɪ)	sie spricht deutlich
she sings unclearly (ʃɪ ˈsɪŋs ˈʌnklɪəlɪ)	sie singt undeutlich
carefully (ˈkeəflɪ)	vorsichtig, sorgfältig
carelessly (ˈkeəlɪslɪ)	unvorsichtig, sorglos

Unit fifteen

1a

unhappy / happy (ʌnˈhæpɪ / ˈhæpɪ)	unglücklich / glücklich
either (ˈaɪðə)	auch nicht / auch kein(e)
money (ˈmʌnɪ)	Geld

1b

play cards (ˈpleɪ ˈkɑːdz)	Karten spielen
look for (ˈlʊk fə)	suchen
print money (ˈprɪnt ˈmʌnɪ)	Banknoten drucken
sell (sel)	verkaufen
lottery (ˈlɒtərɪ)	Lotterie
rob a bank (ˈrɒb ə ˈbæŋk)	eine Bank ausrauben

1c

problem (ˈprɒbləm)	Problem
police (pəˈliːs)	Polizei
win (wɪn)	gewinnen

3a

lady (ˈleɪdɪ)	Dame
dog (dɒg)	Hund
kidnap a poodle (ˈkɪdnæp ə ˈpuːdl)	einen Pudel entführen
ask for (ˈɑːsk fə)	verlangen
thousand (ˈθaʊznd)	tausend
love (lʌv)	lieben
hate (heɪt)	hassen
fantastic (fænˈtæstɪk)	fantastisch
Don't forget! (dəʊnt fəˈget)	Vergiss nicht!

4a

help (help)	helfen
Ask him! (ˈɑːsk ˈhɪm)	Frage ihn!
Ask her! (ˈɑːsk ˈhɜː)	Frage sie!
Don't ask us. (ˈdəʊnt ˈɑːsk ˈʌs)	Frage nicht uns.
Ask them! (ˈɑːsk ˈðem)	Frage sie! (Mehrz.)

4b

dad (dæd)	Papi
buy (baɪ)	kaufen
gold ring (ˈgəʊld ˈrɪŋ)	goldener Ring
invite (ɪnˈvaɪt)	einladen

5

contact (ˈkɒntækt)	Kontakt aufnehmen
midnight (ˈmɪdnaɪt)	Mitternacht

7	open ('əupən)	öffnen
	page (peidʒ)	Seite
	listen to ('lɪsn tə)	zuhören
	tape (teip)	Tonband
	lesson ('lesn)	Lektion
	worm (wɜːm)	Wurm

Unit sixteen

1a	a lot of (ə 'lɒt əv)	viele
	both (bəuθ)	beide
	moped ('məuped)	Mofa
	mustn't ('mʌsnt)	dürfen nicht
	licence ('laisəns)	Fahrausweis

1b	surname ('sɜːneɪm)	Familienname
	first name ('fɜːst 'neim)	Vorname
	address (ə'dres)	Adresse
	date of birth ('deit əv 'bɜːθ)	Geburtsdatum
	type of vehicle ('taip əv 'viːikl)	Art des Fahrzeugs
	motorbike ('məutəbaik)	Motorrad
	engine capacity ('endʒin kə'pæsəti)	Hubraum
	make (meik)	Marke
	signature ('signətʃə)	Unterschrift
	application form (ˌæplɪ'keɪʃn 'fɔːm)	Antragsformular

2a	road sign ('rəud 'sain)	Verkehrsschild
	overtake (ˌəuvə'teik)	überholen
	turn left / right ('tɜːn 'left / 'rait)	links / rechts abbiegen
	straight on ('streit ɒn)	geradeaus

3	go camping ('gəu 'kæmpiŋ)	Zelten gehen
	take (teik)	mitnehmen
	sleeping bag ('sliːpiŋ 'bæg)	Schlafsack
	sleep (sliːp)	schlafen
	don't have to ('dəunt 'hæv tə)	müssen nicht
	ground (graund)	Boden
	spend (spend)	ausgeben
	trip (trip)	Reise
	things (θiŋz)	Dinge, Sachen
	necessary ('nesəsəri)	nötig
	hotel guide (həu'tel 'gaid)	Hotelführer
	map (mæp)	Karte
	passport ('pɑːspɔːt)	Reisepass

4	campsite ('kæmpsait)	Zeltplatz
	list (list)	Liste
	rule (ruːlz)	Regel
	leave (liːv)	verlassen
	by eleven (bai ɪ'levn)	bis elf Uhr
	last (lɑːst)	letzte(r)
	park (pɑːk)	parken
	make a fire ('meik ə 'faiə)	Feuer anzünden

5	partner ('pɑːtnə)	Partner

6	tomorrow (tə'mɒrəu)	morgen

Unit-by-unit word list

Unit seventeen

1a

ticket office ('tɪkɪt 'ɒfɪs)	Billettschalter
Can I help you? ('kæn aɪ 'help ju)	Kann ich Ihnen behilflich sein?
The train leaves at 5. (ðə 'treɪn 'liːvz ət 'faɪv)	Der Zug fährt um 5 Uhr ab.
platform ('plætfɔːm)	Perron, Bahnsteig
fare (feə)	Fahrpreis
single ('sɪŋgl)	einfach
return (rɪ'tɜːn)	retour
first class ('fɜːst 'klɑːs)	erste Klasse
journey ('dʒɜːnɪ)	Reise
Goodbye. (ˌgʊd'baɪ)	Auf Wiedersehen!

1b

pay (peɪ)	bezahlen
reserve (rɪ'zɜːv)	reservieren
find out ('faɪnd 'aʊt)	herausfinden
pack (pæk)	packen
seat (siːt)	Sitzplatz

2a

passenger ('pæsɪndʒə)	Passagier

3a

compartment (kəm'pɑːtmənt)	Abteil
It's a long way … ('ɪts ə 'lɒŋ 'weɪ)	Es ist weit …
pass the time ('pɑːs ðə 'taɪm)	die Zeit vertreiben
out of the window ('aʊt əv ðə 'wɪndəʊ)	aus dem Fenster
opposite ('ɒpəzɪt)	gegenüber
talk (tɔːk)	reden
knit (nɪt)	stricken

4

silver ('sɪlvə)	Silber
gold (gəʊld)	Gold
adult ('ædʌlt)	Erwachsener
valid ('vælɪd)	gültig
travel ('trævl)	reisen
free (friː)	gratis

Unit eighteen

1a

amateur ('æmətə)	Amateur
code (kəʊd)	Code
he's interested in … ('hiːz 'ɪntrɪstɪd ɪn)	er interessiert sich für …
huge (hjuːdʒ)	riesig
all over the world ('ɔːl 'əʊvə ðə 'wɜːld)	auf der ganzen Welt
headphones ('hedfəʊnz)	Kopfhörer
in the middle of ('ɪn ðə 'mɪdl əv)	mitten in

1b

visit ('vɪsɪt)	besuchen
sun (sʌn)	Sonne
shine (ʃaɪn)	scheinen
at the moment ('æt ðə 'məʊmənt)	gerade jetzt
everyone ('evrɪwʌn)	alle, jedermann
warm (wɔːm)	warm
rain (reɪn)	regnen

2a

queen (kwiːn)	Königin
president ('prezɪdənt)	Präsident

2b

banker ('bæŋkə)	Bankier
most people ('məʊst 'piːpl)	die meisten Leute

2c	What's the weather like? ('wɒts ðə 'weðə 'laɪk)	Wie ist das Wetter?
	bad (bæd)	schlecht
	snow (snəʊ)	schneien
	cloudy ('klaʊdɪ)	bewölkt
	windy ('wɪndɪ)	windig
	foggy ('fɒgɪ)	neblig
3a	everything ('evrɪθɪŋ)	alles
	public holiday ('pʌblɪk 'hɒlədɪ)	Feiertag
	wear (weə)	tragen (Kleider)
	suit (sjuːt)	Anzug
	tie (taɪ)	Krawatte
	teach (tiːtʃ)	unterrichten
3b	star (stɑː)	Stern
	uniform ('juːnɪfɔːm)	Uniform
5b	right now ('raɪt 'naʊ)	jetzt gerade

Unit nineteen

1a	go out ('gəʊ 'aʊt)	ausgehen
	bike ride ('baɪk 'raɪd)	Velofahrt
	walk (wɔːk)	Spaziergang
	It's raining cats and dogs. (ɪts 'reɪnɪŋ 'kæts n 'dɒgz)	Es regnet in Strömen.
	subject ('sʌbdʒekt)	Schulfach
	report (rɪ'pɔːt)	Zeugnis
	the worst mark (ðə 'wɜːst 'mɑːk)	die schlechteste Note
	literature ('lɪtərətʃə)	Literatur
	art (ɑːt)	Zeichnen
	geography (dʒɪ'ɒgrəfɪ)	Geografie
	mathematics (ˌmæθə'mætɪks)	Mathematik
	domestic science (dəʊ'mestɪk 'saɪəns)	Haushaltkunde
	history ('hɪstərɪ)	Geschichte
	biology (baɪ'ɒlədʒɪ)	Biologie
	physics ('fɪzɪks)	Physik
	chemistry ('kemɪstrɪ)	Chemie
	better than ('betə ðən)	besser als
	later ('leɪtə)	später
	end (end)	Ende
2a	heavy ('hevɪ)	schwer
3a	quiz (kwɪz)	Quiz
	high (haɪ)	hoch
	mountain ('maʊntɪn)	Berg
	canton ('kæntɒn)	Kanton
	river ('rɪvə)	Fluss
	large (lɑːdʒ)	gross
	town (taʊn)	Stadt
	university (ˌjuːnɪ'vɜːsətɪ)	Universität
	sunny ('sʌnɪ)	sonnig
	pass (pɑːs)	Pass, Passstrasse
4a	island ('aɪlənd)	Insel
	continent ('kɒntɪnənt)	Kontinent
	kilometre ('kɪləʊˌmiːtə)	Kilometer
	square metre ('skweə 'miːtə)	Quadratmeter

Unit-by-unit word list

Unit twenty

1a

north of … ('nɔːθ əv)	nördlich …
south of … ('sauθ əv)	südlich …
airport ('eəpɔːt)	Flughafen
flat (flæt)	Wohnung
look after ('luk 'ɑːftə)	sich kümmern um
Let's go … ('lets 'gəu)	Gehen wir …
have a look ('hæv ə 'luk)	ansehen, schauen
exciting (ɪk'saɪtɪŋ)	aufregend
millionaire (ˌmɪljə'neə)	Millionär
a lot more expensive (ə 'lɒt 'mɔː ɪk'spensɪv)	viel teurer
quiet ('kwaɪət)	ruhig
tourist ('tuərɪst)	Tourist
all year round ('ɔːl 'jɪə 'raund)	das ganze Jahr hindurch
important (ɪm'pɔːtnt)	wichtig

1b

distance ('dɪstəns)	Distanz

2a

at an estate agent's (æt ən ɪ'steɪt eɪdʒənts)	beim Grundstückmakler
fill in ('fɪl ɪn)	ausfüllen
separate ('seprət)	separat
kitchen ('kɪtʃɪn)	Küche
gas (gæs)	Gas
electricity (ˌɪlek'trɪsətɪ)	Strom
bathroom ('bɑːθrum)	Badezimmer
central heating ('sentrəl 'hiːtɪŋ)	Zentralheizung
garage ('gærɑːdʒ)	Garage
basement ('beɪsmənt)	Untergeschoss
ground floor ('graund 'flɔː)	Parterre, Erdgeschoss
price (praɪs)	Kaufpreis
up to ('ʌp tə)	bis

2b

description (dɪ'skrɪpʃn)	Beschreibung

3a

living room ('lɪvɪŋ 'rum)	Wohnzimmer
dining room ('daɪnɪŋ 'rum)	Esszimmer
shopping centre ('ʃɒpɪŋ 'sentə)	Einkaufszentrum
under ('ʌndə)	unter

4

piece of paper ('piːs əv 'peɪpə)	Blatt Papier

Unit twenty-two

1a

party ('pɑːtɪ)	Party, Fest
give a party ('gɪv ə 'pɑːtɪ)	zu einer Party einladen
a week on Saturday (ə 'wiːk ɒn 'sætədɪ)	am Samstag in einer Woche
grandparents ('grænd,peərənts)	Grosseltern
wedding anniversary ('wedɪŋ ˌænɪ'vɜːsərɪ)	Hochzeitstag
What a pity! ('wɒt ə 'pɪtɪ)	Wie schade!
I mean … (aɪ 'miːn)	Ich meine …
What on earth … ? ('wɒt ɒn 'ɜːθ)	Was um Himmels willen … ?
give (gɪv)	schenken
musical ('mjuːzɪkl)	Musical
present ('preznt)	Geschenk
meet (miːt)	treffen
Where shall we meet? ('weə ʃəl wɪ miːt)	Wo sollen wir uns treffen?
I'd prefer … ('aɪd prɪ'fɜː)	Ich würde … vorziehen

1c	babysit ('beɪbɪ,sɪt)	Kinder hüten
2a	twins (twɪnz)	Zwillinge
	neighbour ('neɪbə)	Nachbar(in)
	person ('pɜ:sn)	Person
	camera ('kæmərə)	Kamera
	a bottle of perfume (ə 'bɒtl əv 'pɜ:fju:m)	ein Fläschchen Parfüm
	a box of chocolates (ə 'bɒks əv 'tʃɒkələts)	eine Schachtel Pralinen
3a	If you ever … (ɪf ju 'evə)	Wenn du jemals …
	need (ni:d)	brauchen
	help (help)	Hilfe
	excited (ɪk'saɪtɪd)	aufgeregt
	exact (ɪg'zækt)	genau
	sure (ʃuə)	sicher
	a wonderful time (ə 'wʌndəful 'taɪm)	eine wunderbare Zeit
	ferry ('ferɪ)	Fähre
	after lunch ('ɑ:ftə 'lʌntʃ)	nach dem Mittagessen
	catch a train ('kætʃ ə 'treɪn)	den Zug erreichen
	send (send)	senden
	promise ('prɒmɪs)	versprechen
3b	stadium ('steɪdjəm)	Stadion
3c	boat trip ('bəut 'trɪp)	Schifffahrt
	lake (leɪk)	See
	pizza ('pi:tsə)	Pizza
4	wash ('wɒʃ)	waschen

Unit twenty-three

1a	back (bæk)	zurück
	programme ('prəugræm)	Programm
	hear (hɪə)	hören
	twenties ('twentɪz)	das Alter zwischen 20 und 30
	nurse (nɜ:s)	Krankenschwester
	hard (hɑ:d)	hart, schwierig
	doctor ('dɒktə)	Arzt
	country ('kʌntrɪ)	Land
	perhaps (pə'hæps)	vielleicht
	life (laɪf)	Leben
1b	remember (rɪmembər)	sich erinnern
	still (stɪl)	immer noch
	if (ɪf)	ob
	bus driver ('bʌs 'draɪvə)	Busfahrer
	difficult ('dɪfɪkəlt)	schwierig
1c	easy (i:zɪ)	leicht, einfach
2a	granddaughter ('græn,dɔ:tə)	Enkelin
	grandson ('grænsʌn)	Enkel
2b	banana (bə'nɑ:nə)	Banane
	birthday card ('bɜ:θdeɪ 'kɑ:d)	Geburtstagskarte
3a	yesterday ('jestədɪ)	gestern

Unit-by-unit word list

4a

boring ('bɔːrɪŋ)	langweilig
football match ('fʊtbɔːl 'mætʃ)	Fussballspiel
football player ('fʊtbɔːl 'pleɪə)	Fussballspieler
at the hairdresser's (ət ðə 'heəˌdresəz)	beim Coiffeur
awful ('ɔːfʊl)	schrecklich
other people ('ʌðə 'piːpl)	andere Leute

Unit twenty-four

1a

general knowledge ('dʒenərəl 'nɒlɪdʒ)	Allgemeinwissen
comprehensive school (ˌkɒmprɪ'hensɪv 'skuːl)	Gesamtschule
final ('faɪnl)	Final
the last part (ðə 'lɑːst 'pɑːt)	der letzte Teil
before (bɪ'fɔː)	bevor
correct (kə'rekt)	richtig
astronaut ('æstrənɔːt)	Astronaut
moon (muːn)	Mond
Well done! ('wel 'dʌn)	Gut gemacht!
which (wɪtʃ)	welche(r)
again (ə'gen)	wieder
Second World War ('sekənd 'wɜːld 'wɔː)	Zweiter Weltkrieg
need (niːd)	brauchen
invent (ɪn'vent)	erfinden
electric light (ɪ'lektrɪk 'laɪt)	elektrisches Licht
bad luck ('bæd 'lʌk)	Pech
state (steɪt)	Staat
space shuttle ('speɪs 'ʃʌtl)	Weltraumfähre
land (lænd)	landen
team (tiːm)	Mannschaft, Gruppe
prize (praɪz)	Preis, Gewinn

5a

photograph ('fəʊtəgrɑːf)	Foto
born (bɔːn)	geboren
century ('sentʃʊrɪ)	Jahrhundert
mobile phone (ˌməʊbaɪl 'fəʊn)	Handy
plastic shopping bag ('plæstɪk 'ʃɒpɪŋ 'bæg)	Plastiktragtasche

Unit twenty-five

1a

famous painter ('feɪməs 'peɪntə)	berühmter Maler
move (muːv)	umziehen
paint (peɪnt)	malen
start (stɑːt)	anfangen, beginnen
suddenly ('sʌdnlɪ)	plötzlich
stop (stɒp)	aufhören
artist ('ɑːtɪst)	Künstler
produce (prə'djuːs)	produzieren, verfertigen
hundreds of paintings ('hʌndrədz əv 'peɪntɪŋz)	Hunderte von Bildern
change (tʃeɪndʒ)	sich verändern
die (daɪ)	sterben

2a

story ('stɔːrɪ)	Geschichte
lonely ('ləʊnlɪ)	einsam

2b

moral ('mɒrəl)	Lehre

3a

present ('preznt)	Gegenwart
past (pɑːst)	Vergangenheit

3b

positive ('pɒzətɪv)	positiv
negative ('negətɪv)	negativ

5a

birthplace ('bɜːθpleɪs)	Geburtsort

5b

already (ɔːl'redɪ)	schon
act (ækt)	spielen (Theater, Film)
actor ('æktə)	Schauspieler
someone ('sʌmwʌn)	jemand
murder ('mɜːdə)	umbringen
compose (kəm'pəuz)	komponieren
composer (kəm'pəuze)	Komponist
concerto (kən'tʃeətəu)	Konzert
classical music ('klæsɪkl 'mjuːzɪk)	klassische Musik
politician (ˌpɒlɪ'tɪʃn)	Politiker
general ('dʒenərəl)	General
army ('ɑːmɪ)	Armee

Unit twenty-six

1a

winter ('wɪntə)	Winter
beginner (bɪ'gɪnə)	Anfänger
enjoy (ɪn'dʒɔɪ)	geniessen
very much ('verɪ 'mʌtʃ)	sehr
snow (snəu)	Schnee
beautiful ('bjuːtəful)	schön
sky (skaɪ)	Himmel
save (seɪv)	sparen

1b

project ('prɒdʒekt)	Projekt
record (rɪ'kɔːd)	aufnehmen
parents ('peərənts)	Eltern
plane (pleɪn)	Flugzeug
youth hostel ('juːθ 'hɒstl)	Jugendherberge
hire ('haɪə)	mieten
a pair of skis (ə 'peər əv skiːz)	ein Paar Skis
fall over ('fɔːl 'əuvə)	stürzen, umfallen
try (traɪ)	versuchen
at the same time (ət ðə 'seɪm 'taɪm)	gleichzeitig
ski instructor ('skiː ɪn'strʌktə)	Skilehrer

2a

scarf (skɑːf)	Halstuch
suntan cream ('sʌntæn 'kriːm)	Sonnencrème
woollen hat ('wulən 'hæt)	Wollmütze
sunglasses ('sʌnglɑːsɪz)	Sonnenbrille
warm socks ('wɔːm 'sɒks)	warme Socken
overall ('əuvərɔːl)	einteiliger Skianzug
phrase book ('freɪz 'buk)	Sprachführer
boot (buːt)	Stiefel
glove (glʌv)	Handschuh
goggles ('gɒglz)	Skibrille
stick (stɪk)	Skistock

2b

forget (fə'get)	vergessen

3c

southwest (ˌsauθ'west)	Südwesten

Unit twenty-seven

1a	decide (dɪˈsaɪd)	beschliessen
	department store (dɪˈpɑːtmənt ˈstɔː)	Warenhaus
	multi-storey car park (ˈmʌltɪˌstɔːrɪ ˈkɑː ˈpɑːk)	mehrgeschossiges Parkhaus
	via (ˈvaɪə)	über
	exit (ˈeksɪt)	Ausgang
	lock (lɒk)	abschliessen
	door (dɔː)	Türe
	newsagent's (ˈnjuːzˌeɪdʒənts)	Kiosk
	get out (ˈget aʊt)	aussteigen
	on foot (ɒn ˈfʊt)	zu Fuss
1b	parking space (ˈpɑːkɪŋ ˈspeɪs)	Parkplatz
2a	post a letter (ˈpəʊst ə ˈletə)	einen Brief absenden
	take out money (ˈteɪk aʊt ˈmʌnɪ)	Geld abheben
3a	household department (ˈhaʊshəʊld dɪˈpɑːtmənt)	Haushaltabteilung
	china (ˈtʃaɪnə)	Porzellan
	electrical goods (ɪˈlektrɪkl ˈgʊdz)	Elektrogeräte
	coffee machine (ˈkɒfɪ məˈʃiːn)	Kaffeemaschine
3b	instructions (ɪnˈstrʌkʃnz)	Gebrauchsanweisung
	filter (ˈfɪltə)	Filter
	best quality (ˈbest ˈkwɒlətɪ)	erste Qualität
	satisfied (ˈsætɪsfaɪd)	zufrieden
	brand new (ˈbrænd ˈnjuː)	nagelneu
	perfect results (ˈpɜːfɪkt rɪˈzʌlts)	perfekte Resultate
	guarantee (ˌgærənˈtiː)	garantieren
	aromatic (ˌærəʊˈmætɪk)	aromatisch
	fresh-tasting (ˌfreʃˈteɪstɪŋ)	frisch, schmackhaft
4b	clear (klɪə)	deutlich

A

a 1
about 11
act 25
actor 25
address 16
adult 17
after 22
afternoon 9
again 24
age 6
airport 20
alarm clock 13
all 4
all over 18
alone 12
already 25
always 9
am 1
amateur 18
American 10
an 2
and 2
anniversary 22
answer (n) 24
answer (v) 24
any 13
anything 12
apple 2
application form 16
April 12
are 1
aren't 2
army 25
aromatic 27
arrive 9
art 19
artist 25
ashtray 2
ask 11
ask for 15
astronaut 24
at 1
attractive 13
August 12
aunt 4
awful 23

B

babies 4
baby 3
babysit 22
back 23
bad 18
bad luck 24
badly 3
bag 24
balcony 13
bank 8
banker 18
bar 13

basement 20
basketball 13
bathroom 19
beautiful 26
because 3
bed 13
bedroom 13
bedside table 13
beer 5
before 24
beginner 26
best 11
better 10
bicycle 3
big 3
bike ride 18
biology 19
birth 16
birthday 12
birthplace 25
bit 10
black 1
blind 3
blue 1
boat 22
book 2
boot 26
boring 23
born 24
both 16
bottle 12
boutique 10
box 22
boy 2
boyfriend 8
brand new 27
breakfast 9
bring 12
British 1
brother 4
bus 8
bus driver 23
but 3
buy 15
by (by bus) 8
by (by 11 o'clock) 16

C

cake 12
calculator 5
called 4
camera 22
camp 1
camping 16
campsite 16
can 3
can't 3
canton 19
car 2
card 15
carefully 13

carelessly 13
car park 27
carpet 13
cassette 12
cat 19
catch 22
central 20
centre 1
century 24
chair 2
change 25
cheap 10
chemistry 19
child 4
children 4
china 27
chips 3
chocolate 12
chocolates 22
cigar 8
cigarette 12
cinema 6
city 5
class 2
classroom 2
classical 25
clearly 13
clock 13
cloudy 18
club 13
code 18
coffee 3
cold 13
colour 1
come 11
compartment 17
compose 25
composer 25
comprehensive
  school 24
computer 3
concentrate 13
concert 6
concerto 25
contact 15
continent 19
cook (v) 3
cook (n) 8
correct 24
country 23
cousin 4
crowded 13
cry 3
cup 2
cupboard 13
curtain 13

D

dad 15
dance 3
date 16
daughter 4

day 1
dear 6
December 12
decide 27
department 27
department store 27
description 20
dictionary 5
did 24
didn't 25
die 25
difficult 23
different 6
dining room 20
dinner 8
disc jockey 11
disco 11
distance 20
do 9
doctor 23
does 8
doesn't 8
dog 15
domestic science 19
done 24
don't 2
door 27
drawer 13
dress 10
drink (n) 5
drink (v) 10
drive 3

E

earth 22
east 20
easy 23
eat 3
egg 2
eight 4
eighteen 6
eighth 8
eighty 10
either 15
electric 24
electrical 27
electricity 20
eleven 6
eleventh 11
e-mail 9
end 19
engine capacity 16
England 1
enjoy 26
entrance 2
estate agent 20
Europe 6
evening 2
ever 22
every 9
everybody 2
everyone 18

everything 18
exact 22
excellent 13
excited 22
exciting 20
excuse me 2
exit 27
expensive 10

F

fall over 26
family 4
famous 25
fantastic 15
fare 17
fast 10
fat 10
father 4
favourite 5
February 12
ferry 22
fifteen 6
fifth 5
fifty 10
fill in 20
film 2
film star 5
filter 27
final 24
find 3
find out 17
fine 12
finish 8
fire 16
first 1
fish 3
five 5
flag 1
flat 20
floor 20
fly 3
foggy 18
food 5
foot 27
football 3
footballer 7
for 1
forget 15
fork 2
forty 10
four 4
fourteen 6
fourth 4
France 1
free 17
French 1
fresh-tasting 27
Friday 8
friend 2
from 1

Alphabetical word list

G

garage 20
garden 2
gas 20
general 25
general knowledge 24
geography 19
German 1
Germany 1
get out 27
get up 9
girl 2
give 5
glass 2
glove 26
go 8
goggles 26
gold 15
goldfish 3
golf 13
good 6
goodbye 17
goods 27
go out 19
granddaughter 23
grandparents 22
grandson 23
Great Britain 1
ground 16
ground floor 20
group 3
guarantee 27
guide 16

H

hair 5
half past 9
hamburger 12
happy 15
hard 23
hat 26
hate 15
have 11
have got 4
have to 16
he 1
headphones 18
hear 23
heating 20
heavy 19
hello 1
help (v) 15
help (n) 22
her (poss) 5
her (obj) 15
here 2
high 19
him 15
hire 26
his 5
history 19

hobbies 6
holiday 13
home 13
homework 9
horrible 11
hospital 3
hot 12
hotel 2
house 5
household 27
how 4
huge 18
hundred 10
husband 4

I

I 1
idea 12
if 23
important 20
impossible 13
in 1
instructor 26
instructions 27
instrument 11
interested in 18
interesting 13
international 1
interview 3
interviewer 5
invent 24
invite 15
is 1
island 19
isn't 1
it (subj) 1
it (obj) 10
Italian 1
Italy 1

J

January 12
job 8
journey 17
juice 12
July 12
June 12
just 12

K

kidnap 15
kilometre 19
kiss 6
kitchen 20
knife 2
knit 17
know 2

L

lady 15
lake 22
lamp 13
land 24
language 6
laptop 6
large 19
last 16
later 19
learn 8
leave 16
lesson 15
let's go 20
letter 6
life 23
lift 13
light 24
like 8
list 16
listen 6
literature 19
little 6
live 8
living room 20
lock 27
lonely 25
long 5
look 9
look after 20
look at 13
look for 15
lot 20
lot of 16
lottery 15
love 15
love from 6
lunch 9
lunchtime 11

M

machine 27
make (v) 3
make (n) 16
man 4
manager 3
many 4
map 16
March 12
mark 19
match 23
mathematics 19
may 10
May 12
me 2
mean 22
meet 22
men 4
menu 2
mess 11
metre 13

middle 18
midnight 15
milk 12
millionaire 20
mineral water 12
mini 13
minute 9
mirror 13
mistake 13
mobile phone 24
modern 10
moment 18
Monday 8
money 15
month 3
moon 24
moped 16
moral 25
more 12
morning 9
most 18
mother 4
mountain 19
move 25
Mr 3, Mrs 8
much 10
multi-storey 27
murder 25
music 6
musical (adj) 11
musical (n) 22
must 3
mustn't 16
my 1

N

name 1
near 11
necessary 16
need 22
negative 25
neighbour 22
never 9
new 3
newsagent's 27
newspaper 3
next 3
next to 2
nice 13
night 13
nine 4
nineteen 6
ninety 10
ninth 9
no 1
none 4
north 20
Northern Ireland 1
November 12
now 6
number 4
nurse 23

O

o'clock 6
October 12
of 2
of course 10
office 5
often 9
old 6
on 2
once 9
one 1
only 4
only child 4
open 15
opera 6
opposite 10
or 10
orange 2
order 12
other 23
our 6
out of 17
overall 26
overtake 16

P

pack 17
page 15
paint 25
painter 25
painting 25
pair 26
paper 20
parents 26
park (n) 3
park (v) 16
parking space 27
part 24
partner 16
party 22
pass 19
passenger 17
passport 16
pass the time 17
past 9
pay 17
pen 5
pencil 5
penfriend 6
people 3
per 6
perfect 27
perfume 22
perhaps 23
person 22
phone 3
photo 2
photograph 24
phrase 26
physics 19

picture 13
piece 20
pilot 13
pity 22
pizza 22
pizzeria 12
place 13
plan 2
plane 26
plant 13
plastic 24
plate 2
platform 17
play (v) 3
play (n) 6
please 1
police 15
politician 25
poodle 15
poor 10
pop singer 5
positive 25
post 27
postcard 13
pot 12
pound 10
prefer 22
present 22
president 18
print 15
problem 15
produce 25
programme 23
project 26
promise 22
public 18
pullover 5
put 8

Q

quality 27
quarter past 9
quarter to 9
queen 18
question 11
quick 13
quiet 20
quiz 19

R

radio 5
rain 18
read 3
reading 6
really 13
reception 1
record 26
red 1
remember 23

report 19
reserve 17
restaurant 3
result 27
return 17
rich 10
ride 3
right (≠ wrong) 13
right (≠ left) 16
right now 18
ring 15
river 19
road sign 16
rob 15
room 4
round 20
rubber 5
ruler 5
rules 16

S

salad 12
same 1
sandwich 12
satisfied 27
Saturday 8
saucer 2
save 26
say 12
scarf 26
school 2
Scotland 1
sea 13
seat 17
second 2
secretary 4
see 4
sell 15
send 22
separate 20
September 12
seven 4
seventeen 6
seventy 10
shall 22
she 1
shine 18
shoe 5
shopping 24
shopping centre 20
short 5
shorthand 3
signature 16
silver 17
sing 3
single 17
sister 3
sit 12
six 4
sixteen 6
sixth 6
sixty 10

ski (v) 3
ski (n) 26
skirt 10
sky 26
sleep 16
sleeping bag 16
slow 10
small 10
smile 3
smoke 8
smoky 13
snack bar 2
snow (v) 18
snow (n) 26
so 11
sock 26
some 23
someone 25
something 12
sometimes 9
son 4
soon 11
sorry 2
south 20
southwest 26
space shuttle 24
spaghetti 3
Spain 1
Spanish 1
speak 3
spend 16
spoon 2
square kilometre 19
stadium 22
star 18
start 3
state 24
station 9
stay 13
stick 26
still 23
stop 25
story 25
straight on 16
street 11
student 1
subject 19
suddenly 25
sugar 8
suit 18
summer 1
sun 18
Sunday 8
sunglasses 26
suntan cream 26
sunny 19
sure 22
surname 16
swim 3
swimming 6
swimming pool 13
Swiss 1
Switzerland 1

T

table 2
take 16
take out 27
talk 17
tall 10
tape 15
tea 5
teach 18
teacher 2
team 24
telephone 13
television 3
tell 9
ten 5
tennis 6
tennis court 13
tent 2
tenth 10
than 19
thanks 12
thank you 2
that 4
the 1
their 6
them 15
then 11
there 11
these 6
they 2
thin 10
things 16
think 5
third 3
thirteen 6
thirty 10
this 2
those 6
thousand 15
three 3
Thursday 8
ticket 6
ticket office 17
tie 18
time 6
times 9
to 2
today 6
toilet 2
tomorrow 16
too 1
tourist 20
town 19
train 17
travel 17
tray 2
tree 4
trip 16
trousers 5
try 26
try on 10
Tuesday 8

turn 16
twelfth 12
twelve 6
twenties 23
twenty 6
twice 9
twins 22
two 2
type (v) 3
type (n) 16

U

uncle 4
unclearly 13
under 20
understand 13
unhappy 15
uniform 18
unit 1
United Kingdom 1
university 19
unlucky 13
up to 20
us 15
use 3
usually 9

V

valid 17
vehicle 16
very 3
very much 26
via 27
video 13
view 13
visit 18

W

waiter 12
Wales 1
walk (v) 3
walk (n) 19
want 13
war 24
warm 18
was 23
washroom 2
wasn't 23
waste paper basket 13
watch (v) 3
watch (n) 4
water 12
way 17
we 2
wear 18
weather 13
wedding 22
Wednesday 8

Alphabetical word list

week 9
weekend 20
welcome 2
well 3
were 23
weren't 23
west 20
what 1
when 11
where 1
which 24
white 1
who 5
why 3
wife 4
win 15
window 13
windy 18
wine 5
winter 26
with 2
woman 4
women 4
wonderful 22
woollen 26
word 13
work 8
world 18
worm 15
worse 19
worst 19
would like 12
wouldn't like 12
write 3

Y

year 6
yellow 1
yes 1
yesterday 23
you 1
young 10
your 1
youth hostel 26

Instructions

again (ə'gen)   noch einmal
already (ɔːl'redɪ)   schon
answer ('ɑːnsə)   Antwort / antworten
ask (ɑːsk)   fragen
Ask about … ('ɑːsk ə'baʊt)   Frage über / nach …
Begin with … (bɪ'gɪn wɪð)   Beginn mit …
Begin like this … (bɪ'gɪn laɪk 'θɪs) Fange so an …
below (bɪ'leʊ)   unten / unten stehend
box (bɒks)   Kasten
brackets ('brækɪts)   Klammern
choose (tʃuːz)   wählen
circle ('sɜːkl)   Kreis
combine (kəm'baɪn)   kombinieren
compare (kəm'peə)   vergleichen
complete (kəm'pliːt)   vervollständigen
conversation (ˌkɒnvə'seɪʃn)   Gespräch
correct (kə'rekt)   richtig / korrigieren
correct order (kə'rekt 'ɔːdə)   richtige Reihenfolge
cross (krɒs)   Kreuz
dialogue ('daɪəlɒg)   Dialog
each picture ('iːtʃ 'pɪktʃə)   jedes Bild
ending ('endɪŋ)   Endung
example (ɪg'zɑːmpl)   Beispiel
exercise ('eksəsaɪz)   Übung
false (fɔːls)   falsch
fill in ('fɪl ɪn)   ausfüllen
find (faɪnd)   finden
find out (faɪnd 'aʊt)   herausfinden
following ('fɒleʊɪŋ)   folgend
form (fɔːm)   Form
go with ('geʊ 'wɪð)   zusammenpassen
go together ('geʊ tə'geðə)   zusammenpassen
group (gruːp)   Gruppe
hear (hɪə)   hören
important (ɪm'pɔːtnt)   wichtig
information (ˌɪnfə'meɪʃn)   Information
letter ('letə)   Buchstabe
like (laɪk)   wie
list (lɪst)   Liste
listen to ('lɪsn tʊ)   zuhören
look at ('lʊk ət)   anschauen
Make a dialogue …   Spielt einen Dialog …
   ('meɪk ə 'daɪəlɒg)
Make a report about …   Berichte über …
   ('meɪk ə rɪ'pɔːt)
Make sentences …   Bilde Sätze …
   ('meɪk 'sentənsɪz)
Mark the words …   Markiere die Wörter …
   ('mɑːk ðə 'wɜːdz)
match (mætʃ)   zuordnen
middle ('mɪdl)   Mitte
missing word ('mɪsɪŋ 'wɜːd)   fehlendes Wort
mistake (mɪ'steɪk)   Fehler
Mix the order … ('mɪks ðɪ 'ɔːdə)   Verändere die
                                          Reihenfolge …
negative ('negətɪv)   negativ
next to ('neks tʊ)   neben
Number the words …   Nummeriere die
   ('nʌmbə ðə 'wɜːdz)   Wörter …
opposite of ('ɒpəzɪt əʌ)   Gegenteil von
order ('ɔːdə)   Reihenfolge
partner ('pɑːtnə)   Partner
past (pɑːst)   Vergangenheit

picture ('pɪktʃə) — Bild
positive ('pɒzətɪʌ) — positiv
possible ('pɒsəbl) — möglich
present ('preznt) — Gegenwart
question ('kwestʃən) — Frage
remember (rɪ'membə) — sich erinnern
report (rɪ'pɔːt) — Bericht
sentence ('sentəns) — Satz
short answer ('ʃɔːt 'ɔːnsə) — Kurzantwort
Start with … ('stɑːt wɪð) — Beginne mit …
story ('stɔːrɪ) — Geschichte
table ('teɪbl) — Tabelle
tape (teɪp) — Tonband
Think about … ('θɪŋk ə'baʊt) — Denke über … nach
Think of … ('θɪŋk əʌ) — Suche …
tick (tɪk) — Häkchen (✓)
true (truː) — wahr / richtig
underline (ˌʌndə'laɪn) — unterstreichen
use (juːz) — brauchen
verb (vɜːb) — Verb
word (wɜːd) — Wort
Work in groups … ('wɜːk ɪn 'gruːps) — Arbeitet in Gruppen …

write (raɪt) — schreiben
Write about … ('raɪt ə'baʊt) — Schreibe über …
write down … ('raɪt daʊn) — aufschreiben
Write to Claire. ('raɪt tʊ 'kleə) — Schreibe an Claire.

Geographical names

Aberdeen (ˌæbə'diːn)
Africa ('æfrɪkə)
Alaska (ə'læskə)
Algiers (æl'dʒɪəz)
Amazon ('æməzən)
America (ə'merɪkə)
Australia (ɒ'streɪljə)
Avignon ('ævɪŋɒn)
Bath (bɑːθ)
Belfast (bel'fɑːst)
Birmingham ('bɜːmɪŋəm)
Black Sea ('blæk 'siː)
Bombay (ˌbɒm'beɪ)
Boston ('bɒstən)
Brighton ('braɪtn)
Brisbane ('brɪzbeɪn)
Bristol ('brɪstl)
Britain ('brɪtn)
California (ˌkælɪ'fɔːnjə)
Cambridge ('keɪmbrɪdʒ)
Canada ('kænədə)
Cardiff ('kɑːdɪf)
Casablanca (ˌkæsə'blæŋkə)
Corfu (kɔː'fuː)
Cork (kɔːk)
Cornwall ('kɔːnwəl)
Corsica ('kɔːsɪkə)
Cuba ('kjuːbə)
Dieppe (di:'ep)
Dover ('dəʊvə)
Dublin ('dʌblɪn)
Edinburgh ('edinbərə)
England ('ɪŋglənd)
Europe ('jʊərəp)
Florence ('flɒrəns)
France (frɑːns)
Geneva (dʒɪ'niːvə)
Germany ('dʒɜːmənɪ)
Glasgow ('glɑːsgəʊ)
Great Britain ('greɪt 'brɪtn)
Hamburg ('hæmbɜːg)
Honolulu (ˌhɒnə'luːlu)
India ('ɪndjə)
Ireland ('aɪələnd)
Italy ('ɪtəlɪ)
Jacksville ('dʒæksvɪl)
Land's End (ˌlændz'end)
Las Vegas (ˌlæs'veɪgəs)
Liverpool ('lɪvəpuːl)
Loch Ness (lɒk 'nes)
London ('lʌndən)
Lucerne (luː'sɜːn)
Lugano (luː'gɑːnəʊ)
Madagascar (ˌmædə'gæskə)
Malaga ('mæləgə)
Manchester ('mæntʃɪstə)
Mediterranean (ˌmedɪtə'reɪnjən)
Melbourne ('melbɔːn)
Mont Blanc (ˌmɒn'blɒŋ)
Moscow ('mɒskəʊ)
Mount Kenya ('maʊnt 'kenja)

Newhaven (njuː'heɪvn)
New York (ˌnjuː'jɔːk)
Northern Ireland ('nɔːðn 'aɪələnd)
Nottingham ('nɒtɪŋəm)
Palermo (pə'lɜːməʊ)
Paris ('pærɪs)
Penzance (pen'zæns)
Rabat (rə'bɑːt)
Red Sea ('red 'siː)
Rome (rəʊm)
Russia ('rʌʃə)
Salzburg ('sɑːltsbɜːg)
Scotland ('skɒtlənd)
Southend (ˌsaʊθ'end)
Spain (speɪn)
St. Moritz (snt'mɒrɪts)
St. Tropez (snt'trəʊpeɪ)
Swansea ('swɒnzɪ)
Switzerland ('swɪtsələnd)
Sydney ('sɪdnɪ)
Tunis ('tjuːnɪs)
United Kingdom (juː'naɪtɪd 'kɪŋdəm)
Valencia (və'lensɪə)
Vigo ('viːgəʊ)
Volga ('vɒlgə)
Wales (weɪlz)
Weisshorn ('vaɪshɔːn)
Yangtze-Kiang (jæŋtsɪ'kjæŋ)
York (jɔːk)
Zurich ('zjʊərɪk)

Miscellaneous

Days of the week (unit 8)

Monday ('mʌndɪ)
Tuesday ('tjuːzdɪ)
Wednesday ('wenzdɪ)
Thursday ('θɜːzdɪ)

Friday ('fraɪdɪ)
Saturday ('sætədɪ)
Sunday ('sʌndɪ)

Months of the year (unit 12)

January ('dʒænjʊərɪ)
February ('februərɪ)
March (maːtʃ)
April ('eɪprɪl)
May (meɪ)
June (dʒuːn)

July (dʒuːˈlaɪ)
August ('ɔːgəst)
September (sepˈtembə)
October (ɒkˈtəubə)
November (nəuˈvembə)
December (dɪˈsembə)

The alphabet (unit 10)

a	(eɪ)	n	(en)
b	(biː)	o	(au)
c	(siː)	p	(piː)
d	(diː)	q	(kjuː)
e	(iː)	r	(ɑː)
f	(ef)	s	(es)
g	(dʒiː)	t	(tiː)
h	(eɪtʃ)	u	(juː)
i	(aɪ)	v	(viː)
j	(dʒeɪ)	w	('dʌbljuː)
k	(keɪ)	x	(eks)
l	(el)	y	(waɪ)
m	(em)	z	(zed)

Cardinal numbers (units 4, 6, 10)

1	one (wʌn)	19	nineteen (ˌnaɪnˈtiːn)
2	two (tuː)	20	twenty ('twentɪ)
3	three (θri)	21	twenty-one
4	four (fɔː)	30	thirty ('θɜːtɪ)
5	five (faɪv)	32	thirty-two
6	six (sɪks)	40	forty ('fɔːtɪ)
7	seven ('sevn)	50	fifty ('fɪftɪ)
8	eight (eɪt)	60	sixty ('sɪkstɪ)
9	nine (naɪn)	70	seventy ('sevntɪ)
10	ten (ten)	80	eighty ('eɪtɪ)
11	eleven (ɪ'levn)	90	ninety ('naɪntɪ)
12	twelve (twelv)	100	a hundred (ə 'hʌndrəd)
13	thirteen (ˌθɜːˈtiːn)	101	a hundred and one
14	fourteen (ˌfɔːˈtiːn)	210	two hundred and ten
15	fifteen (ˌfɪfˈtiːn)	1,000	a thousand (ə θauznd)
16	sixteen (ˌsɪksˈtiːn)	2,325	two thousand three
17	seventeen (ˌsevnˈtiːn)		hundred and twenty-five
18	eighteen (ˌeɪˈtiːn)	1,000,000	a million (ə 'mɪljən)

Ordinal numbers (unit 12)

1st	first (fɜːst)	11th	eleventh (ɪ'levnθ)
2nd	second ('sekənd)	12th	twelfth (twelfθ)
3rd	third (θɜːd)	20th	twentieth ('twentɪɪθ)
4th	fourth (fɔːθ)	21st	twenty-first ('twentɪ 'fɜːst)
5th	fifth (fɪfθ)	22nd	twenty-second
6th	sixth (sɪksθ)		('twentɪ 'sekənd)
7th	seventh ('sevnθ)	23rd	twenty-third ('twentɪ 'θɜːd)
8th	eighth (eɪtθ)	30th	thirtieth ('θɜːtɪɪθ)
9th	ninth (naɪnθ)	40th	fortieth ('fɔːtɪɪθ)
10th	tenth (tenθ)	50th	fiftieth ('fɪftɪɪθ)
		100th	hundredth ('hʌndrədθ)

Short forms

aren't (ɑ:nt)	=	are not
can't (kɑ:nt)	=	cannot
didn't ('dɪdnt)	=	did not
doesn't ('dʌznt)	=	does not
don't (dəunt)	=	do not
hasn't ('hæznt)	=	has not
haven't ('hævnt)	=	have not
he'd (hi:d)	=	he would
he's (hi:z)	=	he is / he has
I'd (aɪd)	=	I would
I'm (aɪm)	=	I am
I've (aɪv)	=	I have
isn't ('ɪznt)	=	is not
it's (ɪts)	=	it is / it has
she'd (ʃi:d)	=	she would
she's (ʃi:z)	=	she is / she has
there's (ðeəz)	=	there is
they'd (ðeɪd)	=	they would
they're (ðeə)	=	they are
they've (ðeɪv)	=	they have
wasn't ('wɒznt)	=	was not
we'd (wi:d)	=	we would
we're (wɪə)	=	we are
we've (wi:v)	=	we have
weren't (wɜ:nt)	=	were not
you'd (ju:d)	=	you would
you're (juə)	=	you are
you've (ju:v)	=	you have

Grammar

Present simple: to be (units 1, 2)

I **am**	I'm not	am I?
you **are**	you aren't	are you?
he **is**	he isn't	is he?
she **is**	she isn't	is she?
it **is**	it isn't	is it?
we **are**	we aren't	are we?
you **are**	you aren't	are you?
they **are**	they aren't	are they?

Present continuous (units 17, 18)

I **am** arriving	I'm not arriving	am I arriving?
you **are** arriving	you aren't arriving	are you arriving?
he **is** arriving	he isn't arriving	is he arriving?
she **is** arriving	she isn't arriving	is she arriving?
it **is** arriving	it isn't arriving	is it arriving?
we **are** arriving	we aren't arriving	are we arriving?
you **are** arriving	you aren't arriving	are you arriving?
they **are** arriving	they aren't arriving	are they arriving?

Present simple: have got (unit 4)

I **have got**	I haven't got	have I got?
you **have got**	you haven't got	have you got?
he **has got**	he hasn't got	has he got?
she **has got**	she hasn't got	has she got?
it **has got**	it hasn't got	has it got?
we **have got**	we haven't got	have we got?
you **have got**	you haven't got	have you got?
they **have got**	they haven't got	have they got?

Past simple: to be (23)

I **was**	I wasn't	was I?
you **were**	you weren't	were you?
he **was**	he wasn't	was he?
she **was**	she wasn't	was she?
it **was**	it wasn't	was it?
we **were**	we weren't	were we?
you **were**	you weren't	were you?
they **were**	they weren't	were they?

Present simple (units 8, 9, 11)

I like	I **don't** like	**do** I like?
you like	you **don't** like	**do** you like?
he like**s**	he **doesn't** like	**does** he like?
she like**s**	she **doesn't** like	**does** she like?
it like**s**	it **doesn't** like	**does** it like?
we like	we **don't** like	**do** we like?
you like	you **don't** like	**do** you like?
they like	they **don't** like	**do** they like?

Past simple (units 24, 25, 26, 27)

I arriv**ed**	I **didn't** arrive	**did** I arrive?
you arriv**ed**	you **didn't** arrive	**did** you arrive?
he arriv**ed**	he **didn't** arrive	**did** he arrive?
she arriv**ed**	she **didn't** arrive	**did** she arrive?
it arriv**ed**	it **didn't** arrive	**did** it arrive?
we arriv**ed**	we **didn't** arrive	**did** we arrive?
you arriv**ed**	you **didn't** arrive	**did** you arrive?
they arriv**ed**	they **didn't** arrive	**did** they arrive?

Regular past forms: arrive – arriv**ed**
paint – paint**ed**
kidnap – kidnap**ped**
cry – cr**ied**

Irregular past forms: see separate list below.

Irregular past forms

be	was / were (wɑz / wɜ:)		have	had (hæd)
bring	brought (brɔ:t)		know	knew (nju:)
buy	bought (bɔ:t)		leave	left (left)
come	came (keɪm)		make	made (meɪd)
do	did (dɪd)		meet	met (met)
drink	drank (dræŋk)		read	read (red)
drive	drove (drəuv)		say	said (sed)
eat	ate (eɪt)		see	saw (sɔ:)
fall	fell (fel)		speak	spoke (spəuk)
find	found (faund)		take	took (tuk)
forget	forgot (fə'gɒt)		tell	told (təuld)
get	got (gɒt)		think	thought (θɔ:t)
give	gave (geɪv)		write	wrote (rəut)
go	went (went)			

Unit references to other grammar	
I, you, he, she, it, we, you, they	units 1, 2
my, your, his, her, its, our, your, their	units 1, 5, 6
a / an	unit 2
can / can't	unit 3
why / because	unit 3
book / books, baby / babies, man / men etc.	unit 4
this / that	unit 6
these / those	unit 6
always, sometimes, never etc.	unit 9
don't you? / doesn't he?	unit 9
one / ones	unit 10
would / wouldn't like	unit 12
there is / there are	unit 13
quick / quickly, good / well etc.	unit 13
go / don't go	unit 15
me, you, him, her, it, us, you, them	unit 15
too / either	unit 15
must / mustn't / don't have to	unit 16
tall / taller / tallest, good / better / best etc.	unit 19
interesting / more interesting / most interesting etc.	unit 20
going to do	unit 22
some / any	unit 23